*This book is dedicated to
Tree, Bic, Bunch, and Bopper,
my wife and children.*

Cultural Competence in Recreation Therapy

Working with African Americans, Chinese Americans, Japanese Americans, Hmong Americans, Mexican Americans, and Puerto Rican Americans

Jearold W. Holland, Ph.D.
Associate Professor
University of Wisconsin-La Crosse

Idyll Arbor, Inc.

39129 264th Ave SE, Enumclaw, WA 98022 (360) 825-7797

Idyll Arbor, Inc. Editors: JoAnne Dyer, Thomas M. Blaschko

ISBNs
paper 9781882883943
ebook 9781611580501

Library of Congress Cataloging-in-Publication Data

Holland, Jearold Winston, author.
  Cultural competence in recreation therapy : working with African Americans, Chinese Americans, Japanese Americans, Hmong Americans, Mexican Americans, and Puerto Rican Americans / Jearold W. Holland.
    p. ; cm.
  Includes bibliographical references.
  ISBN 978-1-882883-94-3 (paper) -- ISBN 978-1-61158-050-1 (ebook)
  I. Title.
  [DNLM: 1. Recreation Therapy--methods--United States. 2. Cultural Competency--legislation & jurisprudence--United States. 3. Cultural Competency--psychology--United States. 4. Cultural Diversity--United States. 5. Needs Assessment--United States. WB 556]
  RM736.7
  615.8'5153--dc23
                                                            2014000910

Contents

Preface

Americans enjoy many holidays and celebrations, and some of these contribute to the overall understanding of American culture. Americans value and embrace, either alone or with family and friends, recreation and leisure activities such as a glass of wine in the evening, cheering for and attending their favorite sports teams, enjoying a shower in the evening to relax, taking a summer vacation, barbecuing and fireworks on the Fourth of July, a call to mom on Mother's Day, watching the Super Bowl and its commercials, and gathering with friends and family at Thanksgiving. American culture is also thought to embrace other elements, including a conscientious work ethic, taking pride in the American flag, and so on.

Typical events and prominent celebrations that many Americans observe include New Year's Day, Valentine's Day, Easter, Memorial Day, Mother's Day, Father's Day, Fourth of July, Labor Day, Halloween, Thanksgiving, and Christmas. Each has a particular degree of significance for people with American heritage. For some Americans, these events and celebrations hold very important places in American cultural understanding, while other Americans may find little significance in them.

As Americans, we tend to value many traditions, including our ancestors' contributions and struggles in establishing our nation, a handshake when greeting another person, a look in the eye when conversing with others, a strong work ethic, rugged individualism, democracy, merit, and independence of thought. These fundamental elements and many more encompass aspects of "American Culture."

American culture is important in the lives of Americans. We expect those charged with our care to understand and appreciate the significance of American cultural elements in our treatment and rehabilitation. So when Americans are hospitalized or experiencing disabilities or illnesses, we expect our caregivers to have appropriate understanding of our cultural touchstones and how they might impact the American experience and potential treatment and rehabilitation. For example, at Halloween it is not uncommon for Americans to dress up in elaborate costumes (some comical, some with political significance, some with historical meanings, some scary, and some with fairy tale meanings). Around Halloween, many children and adults bring candy and treats to their schools and workplaces as snacks or to share with others.

On the evening of Halloween, children dressed in costumes go door to door in their neighborhood ringing doorbells, shouting the traditional request, "Trick or Treat." In preparation, most homes will have candy treats ready for the young revelers. Historically, tricks were provided as entertainment for the youngsters, but this is less common today. Nowadays, if the treats aren't provided, the youngsters will sometimes play tricks on the household. To people unfamiliar with Halloween, these actions may seem odd, and participants could be thought of as strange or weird. Individuals may have differences with regard to how they practice Halloween. Only with an adequate understanding of such cultural events and celebrations can a therapeutic recreation caregiver provide the most appropriate assessment, care, treatment, and rehabilitation of the individual.

Acknowledgements

Few books can be written without the assistance and support of competent friends, associates, and assistants. This book is no different. This book represents the culmination of a significant amount of time reading, teaching, pondering, conferring with colleagues, friends, and students. The following individuals assisted with some aspect of the manuscript. Dr. Susan (Boon) Murray, colleague and friend, provided an excellent critique of an early draft of the book. Boon is a very dedicated and wonderful educator. The following therapeutic recreation and recreation management graduate students at the University of Wisconsin — La Crosse (UW-L) provided valuable assistance in research and editorial assistance for the book: Megan Francaviglia, Alan Tomow, Lisa Savarese, Sara Moore, Sara Phipps, and Erinn Kubla. All provided valuable assistance and insight. A special thanks to Megan for the numerous times we discussed and debated the content of the book. At my encouragement, she proved to be one of my best critics; exactly what was needed. Megan provided very thoughtful ideas and suggestions. Thanks to the Department of Recreation Management and Therapeutic Recreation at the UW-L for a one-semester, one-class release-time to work on the book. The release-time accelerated the book's completion time. Tom Schmidt, retired English teacher and friend, provided excellent editorial advice in the early stages of writing. My wife for more than 30 years, Theresa (Tree), has always provided advice and support in my scholarly activity. Tree, thanks for putting up with the many hours that I have been distracted while working on the book. You are the greatest life partner.

Introduction

America has a racially and culturally diverse population. This diversity has been a part of America from its beginning. Native Americans and Mexicans inhabited the lands of America prior to U.S. government inception. European explorers and their descendants came to the United States from many areas of the world including Scandinavia, France, Spain, and England. Africans came primarily as slaves in the eighteenth century. Arabic immigrants arrived in the early 1800s, while many Chinese immigrants came to America in the mid-nineteenth century. Later, more European immigrants came to the U.S. either fleeing persecution and starvation or seeking their fortune. Southeast Asians arrived in the aftermath of the wars in the late twentieth century. As such, the United States has much of its roots — although not without conflict at times — in racial and ethnic diversity. To be sure, immigrants brought with them a rich and plentiful array of cultures from their homelands.

As numerous demographic analysts have predicted, this racial and cultural diversity continues in America (Aponte & Crouch 1995). These predictions have held true, as evidenced in the two most recent U.S. Census reports. In 2000, 75.1% of Americans were classified as white, 12.6% Hispanic or Latino, 12.7% black or African American, and 3.8% Asian (U.S. Census Bureau 2004). More recently, the 2010 U.S. Census reports indicate 72.4% white (Hixon, Helper, & Kim 2011), 16.3% Hispanic or Latino (Ennis, Rio-Vargas, & Helper 2011), 12.6% black or African (Rastogi et al. 2011), and 5.6% Asian (Hoeffel et al. 2012).

Racial categorization and identity can be even more complex than the census data indicates. For example, in the 2010 census, many individuals wrote "other" on census forms when asked to classify themselves by race (more than 21.7 million — or 1 in 14). Further, in depicting the importance and complexity of understanding race, one participant in the survey responded, "I have my Mexican experience, my white experience, but I also have a 3rd identity, if you will, that transcends the two, a mixed experience." He went on to say, "For some multiracial Americans, it's not simply being two things, but an understanding and appreciation of what it means to mixed." (La Crosse Tribune 2012). It becomes apparent that future racial and cultural identification will be more complex, requiring more in-depth analysis.

Aside from this assertion, some forecasters predict even more growth and diversity in the U.S. population as we continue into the twenty-first century, with estimates of an overall 49% population growth by 2050. These estimates indicate that in 2050 the U.S. populatio "could be" 69.4% white (210. 3 million), 24.9% Hispanic/Latino (llion), 14.6% black/African American (61.4 million), and million) (U.S. Dept of Commerce 2004). The data in will be a racially different country in the future. As t evolves in its racial and ethnic diversity (Holland important that human service personnel, includ acquire the knowledge, information, and skills to guide people of different racial, ethnic, and cultural grou

The healthcare profession is transforming at an amaz America. The recreation therapy profession should strive to be a e forefront of this transformation. The emergent growth of the three largest U.S. ethnic groups — African American, Hispanic, and Asian — will challenge recreation therapy personnel. As the country evolves and changes, culturally sensitive services must meet the challenges of the changing society, which will place new demands on the healthcare industry. Individuals within these ethnic groups may have concerns and problems that are culturally different from that of the current majority Caucasian population. Therefore, it is essential that therapeutic recreation specialists receive adequate training for interacting with such diverse individuals. Recreation therapists should gain knowledge of different cultures and their potential issues, along with cross-cultural skills, to be more effective in cross-cultural interactions.

The overall aim of this text is to address pertinent issues regarding therapeutic recreation and rehabilitation for African Americans, Chinese Americans, Japanese Americans, Hmong Americans, Mexican Americans, and Puerto Rican Americans. Although a single text can't address all issues regarding these groups and their recreation, this book brings to light significant historical, recreational, and cultural practices that may impact therapeutic recreation practice. Not all groups with historical roots from Asia ("Asians") or groups whose dominant historical ancestry comes from Spanish-speaking countries ("Latinos" or "Hispanics") are included. Although there are some commonalities among such groups, there are also significant differences that warrant distinctly different methods or approaches for achieving cultural competence.

Another goal of the book is to provide the reader with rationales and suggestions for improving skills and competencies when working with these racial groups. The therapeutic recreation profession must recognize the importance of considering a patient's or client's cultural perspectives in therapeutic recreation practice. If recreation therapists are to respond effectively to the needs of these groups, they must value their client's diversity, provide culturally relevant programs and services, and understand and respect their client's culture, recreation, and leisure. Therapeutic recreation specialists should strive to ensure that all activities, programs, and services are conducted in a manner that is sensitive, respectful, and understanding of the cultural and ethnic diversity of all clients. Such an approach will assist the professional in achieving "cultural competence" — a concept that will be discussed in more detail later.

This book is meant for therapeutic recreation educators who train professionals, recreation therapy practitioners who provide services to different cultural groups, and students preparing to work in the field of therapeutic recreation. A primary goal is to address specific areas for improving therapeutic recreation practice for clients from selected racial and ethnic groups. Through this book, it is hoped that we can find solutions to the areas we address.

Perhaps it will help to explain why cultural competence is important is we look at as example of an American moving to a different culture. Consider the following scenario: Jackson is a 40-year-old African American. Jackson is very proud of his African American heritage. He has been married fifteen years and has four young children. Jackson and his three brothers were raised by their divorced mother in a very close-knit family in one of the poorest ghettos in Atlanta, Georgia. Jackson and his family are devout Southern Baptists. His grandfather was a Baptist minister and his mother raised him in the church. He recently relocated his family to Costa Rica for a promising opportunity as an administrator of a local boxing club facility. Soon after arriving in Costa Rica, Jackson sustained a complete C-5 spinal cord injury (SCI) as the result of an automobile accident. Prior to the SCI, Jackson was a very active person. Growing up in the southeastern U.S., Jackson was a standout high school athlete in football and basketball. Following high school, Jackson enlisted in the Air Force and served for four dedicated years. After the military, Jackson was hired as a fitness instructor at a local gym. He later married his high school sweetheart. The family attended a Baptist church every Sunday.

If you were the Puerto Rican recreation therapist working with Jackson, what important recreation-related cultural information regarding Jackson might you need to consider in his treatment and rehabilitation? In this scenario, in order to provide the most effective treatment and rehabilitation for Jackson, the therapist must understanding several cultural concepts, including American ghettos; the Southern Baptist religion; the history of African Americans; African American culture, traditions, and celebrations; the role of the father in the African American family; American football and basketball; American military service; the responsibilities of Jackson's new vocational position; and

English as Jackson's first language. American recreation therapists have to address similar questions as they work with patients from different cultural backgrounds. Learning the types of cultural questions to ask and how to address them is the primary aim of this book.

The book has two parts. Part I addresses cultural competence issues. These include the concept of cultural competence, legal requirements and professional standards for competence, cultural competence and its place in the education of recreational therapists, and cultural competence in recreational therapy practice. Part II highlights six specific racial or cultural/ethnic groups and important historical dates, basic cultural customs and their impact on recreation therapy, and finally holidays, celebrations, traditions, and recreation practices that might have an impact on professionals who interact with these groups. In order to be more effective, therapeutic recreation specialists should have, at minimum, adequate knowledge of differing cultural traditions and practices as the specialists evaluate and prescribe appropriate activities and programs.

Finally, note that a few terms are used interchangeably throughout the manuscript: blacks and African Americans, therapeutic recreation and recreation therapy, and recreation therapists and therapeutic recreation specialists.

Part I. Cultural Competence Issues

In this section, the construct of the term "cultural competence" is addressed, along with issues regarding culture in America, the importance of client cultural awareness, and cultural incompetence.

1. The Concept of Cultural Competence

The United States is an incredible nation. The nation is a global leader in many areas: generous freedoms; democracy; fantastic entertainment; diverse geography; entrepreneurial innovation; technological innovation; independence; and diversity of thought, religion, and race.

In the U.S., all recreation therapists and healthcare professionals want to increase their chances of success when working with patients and clients. One way that recreation therapists can do so is to become culturally competent. The increasing racial and ethnic diversity in the U.S. will continue to significantly impact the relationship between culture and recreation therapy practice. Consequently, providing the most effective recreation therapy will rely, more now than at any previous time, on cultural competence and effective cross-cultural communication.

When you hear someone say that another person is of the culture of a particular ethnic or racial group, what does that mean? The elements of culture may have varying degrees of significance to different people. However, culture can't be separated completely from the lives of individuals, as evidenced by Juan Gomez-Quinonez in the following quote: "Culture is historically derived, fluid, composed of both positive and negative aspects, and is malleable to conscious action. In domination and resistance, culture is of salient importance. It is inseparably interrelated to the life of a people and their struggle" (Gomez-Quinonez 1977).

Evolution of the Construct of Cultural Competence

Attention to culture is not a new phenomenon. Even during the Civil War, when free blacks joined the Union Army, army officials believed that there were significant cultural differences between the races and subsequently used literate black civilians and soldiers to help the new black soldiers learn to read and write (Wilson 2002). By utilizing blacks as teachers and chaplains, the Union Army tried to effectively bridge the gap between white and black army personnel. The Union Army was attempting to bring the races together so they could work more closely to win the war. In some respects, the Union Army was successful in this endeavor, as the black army personnel were better able to learn the customs of the Union soldiers and work more effectively with them. It was not a quick learning process for the Union Army or the new black soldiers.

Later in America's early history, following the massive influx of immigrants into the U.S. in the late 1800s, health, social, and educational agencies were forced to directly address the cultural issues of these people. However, most social programs fostered acculturation. In acculturation, people considered "outsiders" are encouraged and expected to engage in practices similar to the dominant population. Acculturation refers to the degree to which people from different cultural groups display or adapt to the cultural behavior of the dominant cultural group.

A very different approach from fostering acculturation emerged from the mid-twentieth-century civil rights movement in America. The passage of the 1964 Civil Rights Act and desegregation laws stimulated both dialogue and action in America. As a result, people from different racial or cultural groups have been encouraged not to "melt" or "homogenize" into American culture. As such, many people have embraced with pride their cultural heritages.

We can see this change in the concept of acculturation in some political and religious events. For example, on June 4, 2009, President Barack Obama began his speech addressing Muslims in Cairo, Egypt, with "Assalamu Alaikum," a Muslim greeting meaning "peace to you." Although President Obama is not Muslim, he deliberately began his speech with this greeting as a way to generate a more relaxed and friendly atmosphere with the Muslims in the audience. Although Obama's comment does not illustrate the construct of cultural competence, he was attempting to convey to the Muslims in attendance that he was knowledgeable of a traditional Muslim greeting. Obama was successful in this, as he received a standing ovation after his opening phrase. Similarly, in March 2012, the Pope wore a Mexican sombrero while riding the Popemobile through crowds of thousands of Mexicans in Mexico. The Pope was acknowledging and showing his awareness of Mexican culture, and the Mexicans in attendance loved the gesture. Sometimes, others feel better when those they interact with are better able to connect with them. President Obama and the Pope were attempting to make such connections with the Muslims and Mexicans at these events.

The importance of one's culture cannot be overlooked. In the 2012 Summer Olympics, the first woman from Qatar was allowed to compete for her country. Qatar is a country of 833,283, made up mostly of Arabs, Pakistanis, Indians, and Iranians; 95% of the population is Muslim. Consequently, Muslim is Qatar's official religion. (Hammond 2010). Seventeen-year-old Noor Hussain Al-Malki, a young Muslim woman representing Qatar, qualified to run the 100-meter dash. Rather than participating in the event wearing traditional track and field attire, which most often includes tight-fitting shorts and tops, Al-Malki began the race in clothing acceptable to people of Muslim heritage, which included a head scarf, long sleeves, and long leggings. Al-Malki was adhering to the cultural traditions of her nation and religion. Although most track athletes wear more aerodynamic clothing during a competitive event, she may have had serious cultural consequences if she'd worn traditional track and field clothing. In short, culture played a part in Al-Malki's appearance.

Another example of the importance of culture on individual behavior was Simon Cho, a 2010 Olympic short-track bronze medal speed skater. In an October 6, 2012 *CBS This Morning* interview, Cho admitted that he tampered with the skates of a Canadian competitor prior to a competitive speed racing event. During his interview, Cho indicated that his coach, Jae Su Chun, instructed him to do the tampering. Both Cho and Chun are of Korean ancestry (Chun is a South Korean native and was the U.S. National Team coach). Although Simon and his American team had nothing to gain by tampering (he and his team could not advance any further), Simon indicated that he was compelled to tamper because, as he stated, "In the Asian culture, when an elder (coach Chun) ask you to do something, it's hard not to do it." Consequently, as evidenced by Cho's actions, culture can be an important determinant in individual behavior.

Base Culture in America

Since therapeutic recreation is practiced in Western societies, Western cultural values will dominate the philosophies of recreation therapists. Completely adhering to Western values while working with clients and patients who maintain non-Western values will create difficulty and confusion in the therapeutic process.

One of the most complete lists of white culture characteristics (accepted by some and questioned by others) was devised by diversity consultant and educator Judith Katz. Katz's white culture characteristics include:

- Rugged Individualism (self-reliance, individuals are assumed in control of their environment, independence and autonomy are highly valued and rewarded)
- Competition (be number one, win at all costs, winner-loser dichotomy)
- Action Orientation (master and control nature, must always "do something" about a situation, aggressiveness, and extroversion)

- Decision Making (majority rules when whites have power, hierarchical)
- Communication ("The King's English" rules, written tradition, avoid conflict, don't show emotion, don't discuss personal life, be polite)
- Holidays (based on Christian religions, white history, and male leaders)
- History (Based on Northern European immigrants' experiences in the United States, heavy focus on the British Empire, primacy of Western [Greek, Roman] and Judeo-Christian tradition)
- Justice (based on English common law, protect property and entitlements, intent counts)
- Protestant Work Ethnic (hard work is the key to success, work before play, "If you didn't meet your goals, you didn't work hard enough.")
- Emphasis on Scientific Method (objective, rational linear thinking, cause and effect relationships, quantitative emphasis)
- Status, Power, and Authority (wealth = worth; heavy value on ownership of goods, space, and property; your job is who you are; respect authority)
- Time (adherence to rigid time schedules)
- Future Orientation (plan for future, delayed gratification, progress is always for the best, "Tomorrow will be better.")
- Family Structure (nuclear family — father, mother, 2 or 3 children — husband is the breadwinner and head of household, wife is homemaker and subordinate to husband, children should have own rooms and be independent)
- Aesthetics (based on European culture; woman's beauty is based on blonde, thin "Barbie"; man's attractiveness is based on economic status, power, and intellect; steak and potatoes; "bland is best")
- Religion (Christianity is the norm, anything other than Juedo-Christian tradition is foreign, no tolerance for deviation from single God concept) (Katz 1999).

Although controversial, some of Katz's concepts of white American culture can be difficult to disagree with. For example, competition could seem fairly accurate when we look at the first presidential debate of 2012 between President Barack Obama and his opponent, Governor Mitt Romney of Massachusetts. President Obama was running for re-election, nearing the end of his first four years in office. (It might be important to note that Obama began his reign when the country was not doing well economically and was also still living the aftermath of the September 11 bombing of the World Trade Center in New York City.) After Obama's first four years, it appeared that Americans were ready for a change in presidential leadership; unemployment was relatively high and many Americans were unable to find work. After the televised debate on October 3, 2012, according to most televised news accounts, most Americans felt that President Obama lost the debate. Many Americans felt Obama was not aggressive enough during the debate, while Romney's demeanor was more assertive. In their next televised debate, President Obama appeared much more assertive and confident in his demeanor, and most Americans believed he won that second debate. As such, American culture assumes that to succeed, the winner should and must display assertiveness, confidence, and a win-at-all-cost demeanor, among other things. Consequently, winning is considered an important aspect of American culture. President Obama eventually won re-election. Obviously, many other critical variables must be considered in such a high-level political situation; we don't know for certain how great a role assertiveness played. Yet to many Americans, the appearance of assertiveness and confidence on the part of Obama and Romney played an important part in Americans' views of the most successful participant in the debates themselves.

Today, the more acculturated a client/patient is, the more likely it is that the Western or dominant traditional (Anglo) strategies and assessment tools will be successful with these individuals. Recreation therapists may view acculturation as a predictor of client success. However, if clients retain the language and embrace the cultural customs and characteristics of their home country or cultural group, they may be viewed as having a higher risk of not meeting some traditional recreational therapy goals. It may be wise to consider acculturation as a tool for determining which strategies and assessment tools might be most appropriate for a given person. In this view, recreation therapists are urged to get to know other cultures better in order to determine if a program built around Western cultural values will be the most successful for an individual.

Other American Cultures

Cultural competence is important to all people, regardless of race or ethnicity, and it demonstrates respect and sincerity. Virtually everyone interacts with people from different cultural groups at some time, either in a personal or professional context. A brief professional context example: a recreation therapist at a community center is introduced to a family that recently moved to Wisconsin from Norway. The family's needs include an effective orientation to the area and knowledge of recreational activities for the entire family. The family would love to have some connection to their former home in Norway. After discussing their needs with the family, the recreation therapist researches the family's home area in Norway, looking at the leisure lifestyle in that area and common customs of Norwegians. While researching, the therapist observes that dancing is a favorite pastime for many Norwegians. The therapist acknowledges that the family is unique; just because they originate in Norway does not mean that they will meet all the general characteristics of Norwegians. In the therapist's initial conversation with the family, however, the mother indicated she enjoyed dancing and would like to continue this pastime in Wisconsin. The recreation therapist also recalled that the children have complained about the foods served in Wisconsin restaurants. The family decides it would like to address both of these issues. At their next meeting, the recreation therapist and the family decide to put their goals into action. They meet at a local coffee shop that specializes in Norwegian delicacies, including the kids' favorite, lefse. The recreation therapist produces a list of other local restaurants that serve Norwegian foods, plus the phone number of a local parks and recreation department and a newsletter of community events. Included in the newsletter is a list of dances, including Norwegian dancing and a workshop on ballroom dancing. This brief scenario demonstrates the active role a recreation therapist can take in achieving some degree of cultural competence with others.

As shown above, recreation therapists must be willing to research their client's worldviews, perspectives, beliefs, attitudes, and ways of life. Here are two other brief examples that impact cultural competence: (a) when interacting with Amish people in hospice, it is good to know who is the elder, because the elder typically controls the money needed for equipment and medical supplies; and (b) when interacting with Hmong patients in hospice, remember that there should be no metal on the body at the moment of death. Without such knowledge of Amish and Hmong culture, care providers may make inappropriate patient/client decisions.

With regards to acculturation, recreation therapists must be aware that Western and non-Western cultural values may be different. Aguilera, Daily, and Perez (2008) summarized some of these differences this way:

Cultural Values

Non-Western	Western
Fate	Personal control
Tradition	Change
Human interaction dominates	Schedules dominate
Group welfare	Individualism and privacy
Cooperation	Competition
Formality	Informality
Indirectness	Directness
Modesty	Self-confidence
Extended family	Nuclear family

To be culturally competent, we must first recognize that culture is an important determinant of who we and our clients are. Culture is what we use to construct meaning within our lives. Our cultural perceptions help us to cope with various situations, to interpret means of expression, and to understand and make sense of the world around us.

Quite often cultural competence is limited to celebrations, foods, dances, costumes, and music. Also, some believe that by studying specific individuals like George Washington, Abraham Lincoln, President Obama, Martin Luther King, Jr., Booker T. Washington, Malcolm X, Cesar Chavez, Jennifer Lopez, Confucius, or Bruce Lee we can learn all we need to know about a particular racial or ethnic group. However, cultural competence is much more. It calls for deeper understanding, integration, and appreciation of differences and unique perspectives. Further, it requires understanding what is not working and at the same time realizing that cultural differences should be viewed as opportunities, not threats.

Cultural competence can better be thought of as a set of behaviors, attitudes, and policies that come together and allow professionals to work effectively in cross-cultural situations. Cultural competence requires a reasonable understanding of another person and an accurate comprehension of the many factors that influence another person's being. In order to accomplish such a broad understanding, thoughtful consideration is required in three broad areas: *Diversity Knowledge* (familiarity with a group's cultural expressions, languages, religions, foods, fashions, festivals, celebrations, and so on); *Historical Cultural Awareness* (understanding of a cultural group's present and historical accomplishments and social injustices, while recognizing how these successes, challenges, and inequalities might continue to influence attitudes and behaviors); and *Cross-Cultural Skills* (skills that promote positive interaction among and between cultures).

The skills of cultural competence also include appropriate cultural assessment and interpretation, adequate cultural interventions, and sufficient cross-cultural communication. Consequently, recreation therapists must consider many cultural variables — which calls for increased knowledge and sensitivity — in multiple areas of patient care. For example, an appropriate understanding of nonverbal gestures can go a long way in overcoming language barriers between races and different cultural groups. Consider that a nod can mean a "yes" or a "no" in some cultures. A simple "thumbs up" can be interpreted by Americans as friendly but may be interpreted as an insult to Afghans or as the number five to those of German heritage. Holding the two middle fingers down with the thumb and straightening the index finger and pinky fingers may mean "rock on" in the U.S., or "good luck" in Brazil, or a vulgar insult in Italy. Forming a circle with the thumb and index finger may be interpreted as "OK" in the U.S., while the same gesture may be interpreted as "worthless" in France, or as a vulgar insult in Russia. And while hugs and kisses are considered normal to many Americans as a public greeting, in Japan such close personal contact might be offensive. In essence, the recreation therapist must also consider the context of the gesture (who is gesturing, how, and on what occasion) in determining its cultural appropriateness. Further, Austin (2004) indicated that recreation therapists should continually educate themselves about cultural differences in eye contact, body language, and personal space. Some examples that Austin (2004) noted: White Americans prefer direct eye contact, while Native Americans and Latinos consider it rude or intrusive; Americans turn their heads from side-to-side to indicate "no," while Russians tend to shake their heads up-and-down to indicate "no." And Americans normally keep about an arm's length between them when interacting, while those of Arab descent may prefer a closer distance, and Australian aborigines prefer even more distance than Americans do.

Along with the correct analyzing of gestures and personal space preferences, recreation therapists need to understand differences in communication preferences among different cultures. As CTRS Deb Getz indicated, "Some cultures respect and honor the ability to keep their personal lives to themselves, other cultures place great respect in their elders and difficulty sharing their lives with people older than they are. In other cultures, it is a sign of weakness to be ill; acknowledging illness is much like acknowledging weakness" (Getz 2002, 151). Understanding these areas will impact the nature of cultural competence. Cultural competence does not require the recreation therapist to adopt a different racial or ethnic group's customs or practices. However, it does embrace appropriate knowledge and understanding of a different group's customs, values, and practices.

Cultural competence embraces a number of personal attributes, including

- personal qualities that reflect genuineness, accurate empathy, and the capacity to respond in a flexible manner to a range of possible solutions in client treatment and care;
- a personal commitment to acknowledge that racism and prejudice continue to exist, while understanding that bias often equates to inequality among people;
- a practical knowledge of the impact of class and ethnicity on behavior, attitudes, and values;
- knowledge of the role of language, speech patterns, and communication styles in ethnically distinct communities;
- familiarity with the resources (agencies, people, informal helping networks, research) that can be used on behalf of people from different racial/cultural groups;
- the ability to communicate accurate information on behalf of ethnic people and their communities;
- the ability to openly discuss racial and cultural differences and issues; and
- the ability to differentiate between general stress and stress arising from cultural factors.

Naturally, clients/patients will expect healthcare professionals to be culturally competent. Devine and others (2006) reported, in a study of African American, American Indian, Latino/Hispanic, and Hmong people with diabetes, that participants expressed dissatisfaction and mistrust of healthcare providers. The researchers found that participants felt they would be misunderstood and disrespected, and that they would not have their needs met in the U.S. medical system. The same respondents indicated a preference for practitioners who were respectful, culturally sensitive, and patient with them. Additionally, culturally sensitive care delivery includes becoming aware of personal biases, increasing knowledge about communication patterns, and incorporating folk healers or healing into patient care for some clients.

Client's Cultural Awareness

Yet the area of cultural awareness and sensitivity may not always be as clear-cut as one desires due to issues of bias, prejudice, or discrimination regarding the culture or race of clients and caregivers. Although it may not happen often today, racial prejudice may still be an issue in some facilities. For example, race could be an issue in nursing home care. A 2010 case in Indianapolis, Indiana illustrates the point. Brenda Chaney, a 49-year-old African American Certified Nursing Assistant (CNA) filed a discrimination suit against the nursing home where she was employed because she was not allowed to assist a resident who had indicated that she did not want an African American to care for her (Indianapolis AP, 2010). In the suit, Chaney claims she observed a resident lying on the floor, but Chaney couldn't help the woman up because the woman had left instructions specifying the race of her caregivers. Chaney had to call for a white aide to assist the resident. Federal laws have much to do with a situation such as this occurring. In 1987, Congress enacted the Nursing Home Reform Law to address abuse in nursing homes. In essence, the law states that nursing homes must reasonably accommodate residents' individual needs and preferences. With this legislation, nursing home residents are free to choose their own doctors. In Indiana, the law was interpreted more broadly, indicating that residents could choose "providers of services." Nursing homes can be institutions where racial friction exists due to the ages of residents. Dementia may also be a factor contributing to resident racial bias, as some elderly people with dementia may revert to the prejudices they grew up with. In the Chaney case, the court held that residents or patients can refuse to be treated by a caregiver of the opposite sex, citing privacy issues. However the court said applying that accommodation to the race of the caregiver goes too far.

Notwithstanding bias and prejudice, cultural elements include such areas as beliefs, values, and behaviors while encompassing language, family roles, gender roles, religious beliefs, time orientation, personal space, eye contact, politeness, spirits, eating habits, music, dance, dress, geographic living location, greetings, leisure, recreation, play, decision-making, and many others. Moore and Moos (2003) indicated that there are many dimensions of culture, including the personal values of an individual, a person's world view (how an individual makes sense of life's events), disease etiology (how a person explains the occurrence of illness/disability), time orientation (an individual's concept of time and the importance of time), personal space (the appropriate distance that should be maintained between individuals during socialization), family organization (the person that is most often considered the head of the family), and power structure (a person or group's ability to bring about or resist change).

While some cultural elements may have significant impact on some people, other elements may have limited influence on certain individuals. Additionally, culture can influence beliefs about cause of illness or disability, expectations about what the individual should do about their situation, and the anticipated expectations of others with regard to given situations. When these elements are appropriately addressed in assessment, treatment, and rehabilitation, clients will be more accurately evaluated and cared for in the therapeutic recreation process.

Cultural Incompetence

An important consideration in this process for both clients and caregivers is what could be termed cultural incompetence. Cultural incompetence implies doing something with or to a person that is unacceptable to that individual or to that person's culture, or something that renders that individual unacceptable to members of their culture. For example, the 2012 female Olympian from Qatar mentioned earlier may have encountered significant difficulties after returning to her home country had she not abided by her culture's dress requirements for women.

It is important that all professionals be culturally competent. Culturally competent care has been addressed in a number of other professional fields, including physical therapy and nursing. For example, culturally competent care in nursing involves integrating knowledge, attitudes, and skills to enhance cross-cultural practice (Lenburg et al. 1995; Lattanzi and Purnell, 2006).

Again and importantly, cultural competence indicates acknowledgement and appropriate understanding of other cultures. Culture plays an important part in what we see as acceptable or nonacceptable. For example, what would you think of a recreation therapist who planned a midnight outing to the beach on June 23rd and led patients to jump backwards into the ocean at midnight for good luck? In America, we might perceive this as strange and unacceptable. Culturally, this is very acceptable in Puerto Rico, however. As a cultural tradition, some Puerto Ricans camp out on the beaches on June 23rd and at midnight jump into the ocean as a sign of good luck. Puerto Ricans celebrate this as the Festival of the Day of San Juan. As another example, a therapist working with Puerto Rican children may take them on January 5th to a park to cut and gather fresh green grass in a box, and then later remind the children to place the boxes under their beds before going to sleep. In many areas in Puerto Rico, people place these boxes under their beds in celebration of the Epiphany (Three Kings Day). The boxes represent offerings to the Three Kings so their camels have feed for their long journey to the Middle East while the Kings leave their own gifts. These are two examples of how culture influences activities, behaviors, and beliefs.

Further, cultural competence implies that effective strategies should be developed to target different racial groups. In sports advertising, such strategies have been successfully used. Armstrong (1998) conducted a study on marketing sports equipment to black consumers. Armstrong proposed that among other strategies, companies a) employ a culturally based approach for marketing to black consumers, b) involve the black media, and c) demonstrate concern and respect for the black community. The results of the study suggested that "Blacks patronage of Nike products may be directly correlated with the efforts Nike has made to communicate with the black consumers" (Armstrong 1998, 16). In these efforts, it is implied that organizations need to reach out to celebrate cultural nuances, celebrations, emotions, and interactions that occur within the target community. Communicative efforts similar to these could be employed by recreation therapists as they work with clients from other cultures.

Without cultural competence, professionals cannot effectively interact with individuals from different racial and ethnic groups and expect that these people will truly understand them and what they are trying to achieve. Without cultural competence, recreation therapists cannot effectively understand others' hopes, frustrations, and aspirations, nor can they grasp the unique histories and appreciate the play, recreation, and leisure of those they serve. Although the therapeutic recreation profession, like all professions, is grounded in specific professional standards and focused on the masses, the masses have been and are rapidly changing. As the masses continue to change, it is prudent to be more mindful of the "new" masses.

In conclusion, cultural competence should be thought of as a process and not an event. Because cultures continually evolve, we might never achieve "complete" cultural competence. Campinha-Bacote (1998) and Purnell and Paulanka (1998) identified four stages of cultural competence that relate directly to a healthcare professional's level of sensitivity regarding interactions with patients/clients from diverse cultural or ethnic groups:

1. Unconscious incompetence, in which the professional is not aware that cultural differences exist; essentially, being "culturally blind." For example, when a professional assumes that all African American

clients share similar values, beliefs, and practices. "They are all alike" reflects this kind of thinking.

2. Conscious incompetence is realizing that cultural differences do exist and being aware that we lack knowledge about another culture.

3. Conscious competence is the deliberate act of learning about a patient's culture, verifying generalizations, and providing culturally relevant interventions.

4. Unconscious competence. During this last stage, the professional clearly demonstrates the ability to automatically provide culturally congruent services to patients/clients from diverse cultural groups.

Whether or not the recreation therapist works directly with clients from different racial groups, diversity training that aids in acquiring cultural competence is still required. Some practicing therapeutic recreation personnel have recognized this need. For example, in a study of rehabilitation staff in Illinois of 80% recreation therapists and 20% art, music, and dance therapists, Linda McCabe Smith and Marjorie Malkin reported that diversity training was tied as the highest-rated training need in inpatient mental health facilities (McCabe Smith & Malkin 1999).

Finally, consider ethics and its relationship to cultural competence. Considering that ethics deals with providing what is best or most appropriate for someone else, not becoming culturally competent could be considered a professionally unethical practice.

2. Legal Requirements and Professional Standards

Standards for cultural competence have been established by several organizations, as we will see here. It may be judicious for the recreation therapy profession to also recommend specific standards for cultural competence. We will look at what has been done so far and what still needs to be done in recreational therapy.

The Joint Commission

In 2010, The Joint Commission (TJC), formerly the Joint Commission on Accreditation of Healthcare Organizations (JCAHO), which accredits and certifies more than 18,000 healthcare organizations and programs in the United States, announced new standards to improve patient care with *Advancing Effective Communication, Cultural Competence, and Patient- Family-Centered Care: A Roadmap for Hospitals* (The Joint Commission 2010). The *Roadmap* discusses significant research on how populations experience decreased patient safety, poor health outcomes, and lower-quality care based on race, ethnicity, language, disability, and sexual orientation. The *Roadmap* states, "Additional studies show that incorporating the concepts of cultural competence and patient- and family-centeredness into the care process can increase patient satisfaction and adherence with treatment." (The Joint Commission 2010, 1). In 2012, TJC began grading healthcare organizations on the new competencies. The *Roadmap* indicates that healthcare organizations will be evaluated in six domains: admissions, assessment, treatment, end-of-life care, discharge and transfer, and organizational readiness. Much of the *Roadmap* requires improving effective communication in these six domains.

National Standards for Culturally and Linguistically Appropriate Services

The Joint Commission built its standards, in part, on the National Standards on Cultural and Linguistically Appropriate Services (CLAS) released by the U.S. Department of Health Human Services Office of Minority Health in 2001. Table 1 lists the fourteen CLAS standards.

Table 1. Cultural and Linguistically Appropriate Services Standards

Standard 1

Health care organizations should ensure that patients/consumers receive from all staff members effective, understandable, and respectful care that is provided in a manner compatible with their cultural health beliefs and practices and preferred language.

Standard 2

Health care organizations should implement strategies to recruit, retain, and promote at all levels of the organization a diverse staff and leadership that are representative of the demographic characteristics of the service area.

Standard 3

Health care organizations should ensure that staff at all levels and across all disciplines receive ongoing education and training in culturally and linguistically appropriate service delivery.

Standard 4

Health care organizations must offer and provide language assistance services, including bilingual staff and interpreter services, at no cost to each patient/consumer with limited

English proficiency at all points of contact, in a timely manner during all hours of operation.

Standard 5
Health care organizations must provide patients/consumers in their preferred language both verbal offers and written notices informing them of their right to receive language assistance services.

Standard 6
Health care organizations must assure the competence of language assistance provided to limited English proficient patients/consumers by interpreters and bilingual staff. Family and friends should not be used to provide interpretation services (except on request by the patient/consumer).

Standard 7
Health care organizations must make available easily understood patient-related materials and post signage in the languages of the commonly encountered groups and/or groups represented in the service area.

Standard 8
Health care organizations should develop, implement, and promote a written strategic plan that outlines clear goals, policies, operational plans, and managerial accountability/oversight mechanisms to provide culturally and linguistically appropriate services.

Standard 9
Health care organizations should conduct initial and ongoing organizational self-assessments of CLAS-related activities and are encouraged to integrate cultural and linguistic competence-related measures into their initial audits, performance programs,

patient satisfaction assessments, and outcomes-based evaluations.

Standard 10

Health care organizations should ensure that all data on the individual patient's/consumer's race, ethnicity, and spoken and written language are collected in health records, integrated into the organizations management information systems, and periodically updated.

Standard 11

Health care organizations should maintain a current demographic, cultural, and epidemiological profile of the community as well as a needs assessment to accurately plan for and implement services that respond to the cultural and linguistic characteristics of the service area.

Standard 12

Health care organizations should develop participatory, collaborative partnerships with communities and utilize a variety of formal and informal mechanisms to facilitate community and patient/consumer involvement in designing and implementing CLAS-related activities.

Standard 13

Health care organizations should ensure that conflict and grievance resolution processes are culturally and linguistically sensitive and capable of identifying, preventing, and resolving cross-cultural conflicts of complaints by patient/consumers.

Standard 14

Health care organizations are encouraged to regularly make available to the public information about their progress and successful innovations in implementing the CLAS standards and provide public notice in their communities about the availability of this information. (U.S. Department of Health and Human Services Office of Minority Health, 2007)

Developmental Disabilities and Bill of Rights Act of 2002

The Developmental Disabilities and Bill of Rights Act of 2002 (Public Law 106-402) defines cultural competence with respect to three broad areas: services, supports, and assistance. In accordance with this legislation, culturally competent services should be responsive to the beliefs, interpersonal styles, attitudes, languages, and behaviors that have the greatest likelihood of ensuring maximum acceptance and participation from culturally different individuals. The act proclaims that such services should be provided in a manner that demonstrates respect for individual dignity, personal preference, and cultural differences (Developmental Disabilities and Bill of Rights Act of 2002). As such, promoting cultural competence among healthcare professionals will assist with issues such as distrust of the medical community and cultural stereotyping of minority patients/clients.

Again, the terms used in the competence area are varied and may include "culturally effective." Cultural effectiveness can be a broad concept and may occur at the personal and institutional levels. Although this book is aimed at issues at the personal level, cultural effectiveness at the institutional level is also important, and may address issues such as:

- Are people from different ethnic groups represented in management and key administrative roles in the organization?
- Have board members and higher-level administrative personnel received cultural diversity training?
- Are there references to cultural diversity in the agency mission statement ?
- Are there volunteers from various ethnic groups?
- Does the agency have plans for recruiting ethnically diverse personnel?

- Do staff from different ethnic groups work cooperatively?
- Is there overt (or an undercurrent of) racial or ethnic group tension permeating staff relationships in the agency?
- Are aspects of different "surface cultures" (food, wall decorations, art, music, music, magazines, celebrations, and so on) reflected in the agency?
- Do brochures, web sites, and other agency communications reflect a diverse service agency?
- Does the agency have collaborative working relationships with other ethnic organizations or influential ethnic group people?

Therapeutic Recreation Standards

The CLAS standards, TJC's *Roadmap*, and the Developmental Disabilities and Bill of Rights Act are useful because they address what professional organizations should do to address cultural proficiency. While the recreation therapy profession has not developed, within its professional practice standards, stronger guidelines similar to the CLAS standards, it has made some strides in addressing diversity.

ATRA has a 2006 board-approved Statement on Diversity which says, "The American Therapeutic Recreation Association (ATRA) has an ongoing commitment to advancing diversity within the field of therapeutic recreation. We acknowledge that diversity includes any aspect of an individual that makes him or her unique. Our association values and actively promotes diverse and inclusive participation by its leaders, members, and affiliates. Further, the association works to educate its membership about diversity issues, and to foster an environment that acknowledges the contributions of all its members. We value the role that diversity plays in every aspect of service delivery, recognizing that diversity is vital to all elements of recreational therapy practice and education." (American Therapeutic Recreation Association 2008). Further, ATRA has twelve *standards of practice,* but none directly mentions cultural competence or diversity. At the same time, ATRA alludes to some aspects of cultural diversity and awareness in the

ATRA Patient's/Client's Bill of Rights when it states, "As the patient/client of therapeutic recreation services, you have the right to

1. Receive appropriate care that respects you as a person and maintains your dignity regardless of race, color, creed, gender, sexual orientation, age, disability/disease, social and financial status, and

2. Receive information in understandable terms about your strengths and limitations identified through an assessment process that is sensitive to your developmental, cultural, and individual lifestyle qualities and characteristics" (American Therapeutic Recreation Association 2000, 93).

Also, the National Council for Therapeutic Recreation Certification (NCTRC) has only one item identified in its 2007 Job Task Analysis Report of knowledge that mentions diversity, in the Required Knowledge Area for CTRS (Foundational Knowledge), where it acknowledges "Diversity Factors" (e.g., social, cultural, educational, language, spiritual, financial, age, attitude, geography) (National Council for Therapeutic Recreation Certification 2007). It is apparent from these observations that additional attention to standards of practice and cultural competence is needed in the therapeutic recreation profession.

Other researchers have identified key cultural competence variables from the individual perspective with respect to knowledge, skills, and attitudes. For example, Vawter et al. (2003) identified nine areas of learning for cultural proficiency for practitioners:

1. Being aware of the influence of culture on health status, beliefs, practices, and values. (Appreciating the fact that culture influences people's health status and shapes their concepts of health, illness, healing, and helping practices.)

2. Increasing self-awareness about your own health beliefs, practices, and values. (Identifying your beliefs about illness/disability causation, prevention, and treatment.)

3. Learning about the prevailing health beliefs, practices, and values of the cultural groups you serve. (Identifying past and present contextual influences, e.. politics, economics, religion, geographic location, family structure, as they impact cultural beliefs.)

4. Identifying potential areas of congruity and difference between your own health beliefs, practices, and values and those of the cultural groups you serve.

5. Increasing self-awareness about your cross-cultural health care ethics. (Consideration of your perception of what the concept of a good cross-cultural relationship entails. Does this imply a trusting and respectful relationship and that the patient/family and the provider agree on interventions?)

6. Learning skills to identify, evaluate, and respond to cross-cultural ethical conflicts, with special attention to challenges to professional integrity. (Distinguishing practitioner objections to patient/treatment wishes based on personal practitioner beliefs.)

7. Developing attitudes culturally responsive to the groups you serve. (Being open-minded and nonjudgmental with patience and empathy.)

8. Learning communication skills culturally responsive to the groups you serve. (An awareness and demonstration of greetings, acceptable amounts of eye-contact, facial expressions, voice tone, sensitive topics, etc. as they relate to the groups you serve.)

9. Developing skills in applying culturally responsive knowledge, skills, and attitudes to particular relationships. (Carefully listening, understanding, and respecting a patient/consumer's perspective on a given topic.)

As can be determined from these proficiency areas, cultural competence begins with an assessment of our own cultural values and subsequently requires an understanding of similarities and differences between cultural groups. Someone who is culturally competent recognizes that racial and ethnic groups may be different in the perception and use of time, the conception of team versus individual, uses of language, patterns of communication, leisure preferences and values, and so on, while acknowledging that these groups are not different in terms of intellectual, physical, or emotional abilities and needs (Jordan 1999).

In many ways, traditional rehabilitation wisdom is to treat everyone the same and not discriminate. While discrimination should never be tolerated, it is not always best to treat all clients the same without considering their racial and cultural backgrounds. These differences must be acknowledged, understood, and accounted for in order to provide the best services for an individual.

3. Cultural Competence in Recreational Therapy Education

The issue of cultural competence in colleges and universities has three major components: the cultural diversity of the faculty, the emphasis on cultural diversity in the curriculum, and the cultural diversity of the students in the program. Each of these aspects needs to be addressed to insure the adequate teaching of cultural competence in recreational therapy education.

Faculty

Faculty members of color remain a small part of the professoriate. Turner and Meyers (2000) in their book *Faculty of Color in Academe: Bittersweet Success* present insightful information on the underrepresentation of minority faculty in higher education. Turner and Meyers observed a continued pattern of limited numbers of minority faculty in higher education institutions, in addition to the persistence of a "chilly" climate for faculty of color in many colleges and universities. In addition, Trower and Chait (2002) reported that whites constituted approximately 95% of all faculty members in 1983, and 83% in 1997. While there has been some small improvement, the majority of the increase in minority faculty is attributed to Asian Americans. At 7.8%, Asian Americans occupy a larger percentage of higher education faculty than African American (5.9%) and Hispanic (4.3%) faculty (Trower & Chait 2002).

Although there is underrepresentation among faculty of color in U.S. higher education, this section will focus on important implications for professional diversity in recreation therapy as it relates to one particular minority group, African Americans, from the perspectives of educators, students, and practitioners. While this section specifically addresses African Americans, similar associations and implications may be made with faculty of other racial and ethnic cultural groups.

Although recreation therapy is a relatively young professional field when compared to many other health-related fields, it is nonetheless important that the profession aggressively addresses a major issue facing virtually all health-related fields: the underrepresentation of minority group people within its ranks. The same issue can be said to be of concern for many other professional fields. Minority physicians are representative of this disparity. For example, the U.S. Surgeon General Dr. Regina Benjamin indicated that the nation needs to step up efforts to increase the number of minority physicians. Dr. Benjamin indicated that minority physicians are only 6% of the total number of U.S. doctors. Speaking at a conference on healthcare disparities about this underrepresentation, Dr. Benjamin said, "There is something wrong with that." A century ago, the percentage of minority physicians was also 6% — the same percentage as in 2004 (Associated Press 2009).

When comparing data from the U.S. Census Bureau and practicing professionals in the recreation therapy profession, it is apparent that there is underrepresentation of minorities in the profession. Data from the NCTRC confirmed this assertion when in 2007 it revealed the racial make-up of Certified Therapeutic Recreation Specialists (CTRS) as 90% white, 5.6% black/African American, 1.6% Hispanic/Latino, and 1.6% Asian/Pacific Islander (National Council for Therapeutic Recreation Certification, Job Analysis Report 2007. If this underrepresentation problem continues in therapeutic recreation, a significant proportion of the population may not be able to contribute significantly to the productive life of all people served.

As noted earlier, educational and demographic forecasters predict a significant increase in minority group people in the U.S. (Pallas, Natrillo, & McDill 1989). Consequently, more and more members of these groups continue to seek higher education. If higher education is to adequately address the underrepresentation problem, fields of study within academia should, collectively and individually and with sufficient commitment, address this issue. It is important that each field of study demonstrate how racial diversity can and will impact professional practice and how underrepresentation of African Americans and other minority groups within its fields may have pungent effects on the profession and on its professional practice.

Broad participation of African Americans in institutions of higher education remains a difficult but necessary problem. This problem has continued for years. For example, Brown (1988) reported, despite the promulgation of affirmative action plans of the 1970s, black full-time positions in higher education decreased during from 1977 to 1983. Brown (1998) observed the impact of minority underrepresentation in traditionally white higher education institutions and found blacks in only 2.3% of the full-time faculty positions in the 1970s and 1980s. Higher education has made some progress increasing the numbers of African Americans in faculty positions; however, there is still room for improvement. African Americans represent about 13 percent of the U.S. population, but comprise less than 7% of all faculty at American colleges and universities (Blake & Gilbert 2010). Further, the Chronicle of Higher Education's *Almanac of Higher Education 2010* reported the makeup of faculty at all higher education institutions in the U.S. as 78.1% white, 5.5% black, 3.6% Hispanic, 7.8% Asian, and 0.5% American Indian (The Chronicle of Higher Education 2010).

The need for more African American faculty has been stressed in important earlier national reports such as *A Nation at Risk* and *One Third of a Nation* (American Council on Education 1983, 1988). These reports have emphasized the need for more African American and other minority involvement in teaching, and have urged an increase in the number of blacks in all aspects of education.

Data from the U.S. Department of Education found that all minority faculty combined (African American, Asian, American Indian/Alaskan, and Hispanic) accounted for 13.4% of all higher education faculty, while whites accounted for 89.3%. (Hispanics may also be counted in a racial category, usually white.) It's important to note that many minority educators hold positions in two-year institutions or may be in non-tenured positions at four-year institutions. Also, few if any two-year institutions have programs in recreation therapy. Even more drastic, at the start of the twenty-first century, only 8% of the parks, recreation, and leisure studies programs in the U.S. and Canada had any minority educators in the tenure-track or tenured (Hibbler 2002).

Recreation and leisure educators also have underrepresentation issues. Bialeschki (1992) reported that the representation of people of color in recreation has been and remains small, which has implications for diversity and multicultural professional practice.

What are some of the potential consequences of such underrepresentation? A lack of minority (people of color) recreation educators in particular may have negative effects when addressing diverse cultural perspectives in recreation courses. Many minority educators have, or have had, interest in multicultural issues, but the small number of minority educators in recreation may mean limited attention to multicultural issues in the classroom and in the literature in the profession. This in turn may lead to fewer minority students preparing to enter the field, as some minority students are influenced by diversity perspectives in their educational studies.

As is the case in most fields of study in higher education, African American faculty members are somewhat scarce in therapeutic recreation. It is difficult to obtain exact statistics on the number of African American therapeutic recreation faculty members, but the American Therapeutic Recreation Association (ATRA) had a total membership in April 1991 of 1,819 members. Of that total, 200 individuals identified themselves as members of a minority group. The number of minority ATRA members specifically categorized as faculty, practitioners, or students is difficult to obtain. At best, the total minority membership of 200 was approximately 11% of 1,819. To some, this figure may be considered an adequate representation of minority involvement in ATRA. However, this number includes other racial/cultural groups in the recreation therapy profession. Even at best, without an accurate count of Native Americans, Hispanic Americans, and Asians Americans, we can't assume a racially representative professional membership. Moreover, in 2007, 4,667 certified therapeutic recreation specialists participated in a job analysis study conducted by the NCTRC. In this study, using a 43.6% sample population, NCTRC reported its racial distribution to be 90.0% white, 5.6% African American, 1.2% Asian/Pacific Islander, 1.6% Hispanic/Latino, 0.2% American-Indian/Alaskan Native, 0.1% East Indian, 0.9% Multi-racial/Multi-ethnic, while eight individuals did not respond to the race question (National Council for Therapeutic Recreation Certification, Job Analysis Report 2007). When these percentages are analyzed more closely, one must realistically concede that the vast majority of the 4,667 CTRS are practitioners and not faculty.

Finally, though more subjectively, contact with faculty in the profession seems to show an underrepresentation problem. At the last few national, regional, state, or local conferences or symposiums for recreation therapy, how many people could be identified as African American faculty? Similarly, for those educated in therapeutic recreation, remember your days as a student majoring in therapeutic recreation or a related field. How many African American faculty teachers did you have? It would appear, given the limited data from ATRA and NCTRC and the more subjective data, that the African American faculty underrepresentation problem has indeed impacted the therapeutic recreation profession, suggesting an important diversity issue for the field: increasing African Americans and other ethnic groups in faculty positions. The profession along with colleges and universities should investigate efforts to increase faculty diversity in four-year colleges and universities.

What can be done to increase African Americans and other minority group people in faculty positions? This is truly a difficult problem, and higher education institutions have attempted various methods. To be sure, nothing has proven to be 100% successful. Strategies could include mentoring undergraduate and graduate students towards pursuing academic careers; inviting minority professors as visiting faculty; "grow-your own" programs, where universities support minority graduate students and instructors without terminal degrees to pursue terminal degrees; and developing cooperative relationships with historically minority institutions that offer undergraduate degrees in related fields of study.

Beyond increasing the proportionality of the actual numbers, is there a specific need for more African American and other ethnic faculty in therapeutic recreation? There's no simple answer, yet the answer is ultimately affirmative. If we take a broad look at the field, the clients served, and the facilities that employ recreation therapists, the justifications are more apparent.

As is the case in most fields in higher education, faculty members (generally considered prominent researchers and leaders in the field) tend to provide direction and focus on specific agendas for those practicing in the field. Faculty members often write textbooks and are generally seen as leaders in the advancement of a profession. The lack of African Americans in faculty positions may have serious effects on professional advancement as it relates to diversity. African American faculty and researchers, due to their backgrounds and experiences, may be more inclined to research issues affecting or related to African Americans and other racial groups. Much of the needed research related to African Americans in recreation therapy — of which there is relatively little to date anyway — may not be attempted.

Second, there is a paucity of research in African Americans and recreational therapy. Many non-minority faculty may be reluctant to write about and research an area they don't understand or don't feel comfortable in. As a result, critical issues that affect blacks as a cultural group may not be sufficiently addressed. If significant research on African Americans in recreation therapy is to meaningfully evolve, it is important to recruit and maintain African Americans or others with diversity research agendas in faculty positions.

Third, as we continue into this millennium, it is critical that the profession better prepare itself for a more multicultural society. Due to the predicted increase of minority populations in the U.S., there will be more culturally different individuals served by recreation therapists. Consequently, it is important to have faculty who are more knowledgeable and sensitive to the needs of these clients in order to better prepare students to serve them.

Fourth, a lack of African Americans in teaching faculty positions can have potential effects on both majority and minority students in higher education majoring in recreation therapy. White students not having access to African American faculty in the classroom could mean that white students don't obtain broad enough cultural or racial perspectives on social or cultural issues for African Americans in recreation therapy practice.

Although white faculty and faculty from different racial and ethnic groups may address multiculturalism as it relates to African Americans, black faculty may provide a broader and more accurate viewpoint of these issues, having experienced these life issues and events firsthand. If students are to be their most effective in working in a multicultural society, they must be provided with faculty — other than white faculty — inclined to present the profession and the world from a multicultural perspective.

Fifth, the values inherent in recreation therapy are reflected in beliefs, characteristics, and qualities such as an acceptance of individual differences, a humanistic concern for the welfare of all people, and diversity with respect to improvement of and involvement in the quality of life for all. While these qualities are central to a philosophical understanding of the profession, therapeutic recreation may not achieve its best successes with African Americans without more faculty diversity.

While this section looked specifically at the African American perspective, the same statements could be made about every ethnic/racial group. It is unlikely that the limited faculty size in an individual recreation therapy program will ever be able to appropriately represent all cultures. However, as a profession, recreation therapy needs to address these issues to ensure that when we add up the ethnic and cultural identities of faculty numbers in all of the training programs, it approximates the identities of the people being served.

Curriculum

In this section, we will look at how multicultural education can be incorporated into the recreation curriculum. First, we'll address the concepts of multiculturalism and multicultural education in the U.S. Second, we will comment on the status and values of multicultural education in higher education. Third, we'll focus on criticisms and prominent curricular patterns in higher education. Finally, we'll discuss the infusion of multicultural education in the core recreation therapy curriculum.

The progress made toward increasing racial diversity at the university level has been challenging, slow, and at best sporadic. Although universities can play an important role in instituting diverse educational perspectives, initiating this type of change has been difficult. The traditional successes of the modern university are, in part, responsible for much of this difficulty and, at times, for much resistance. Higher education institutions have been structured to resist rapid and undesired change (Shils 1982). These institutions are structured so they can buffer and protect their cores — one of the cores being traditional liberal education — against nontraditional initiatives. Buffering allows institutions to absorb and cope with "environmental uncertainty" (Aldag & Sterns 1991). Multicultural education and multiculturalism may be viewed by some as environmental uncertainties not associated with the traditional educational canons in American higher education.

"People learn the values, beliefs, and stereotypes of their community cultures. Although these community cultures enable individuals to survive, they also restrict their freedom and ability to make critical choices and to take actions to help reform society" (Banks 1994, 1). A multicultural education should help students and practitioners view the world from frames different from the ones they generally use. Multicultural education takes into consideration and gives significant and equitable tribute to differing attributes that have had an impact on the development of the modern western world.

Some university faculty members believe that multicultural education benefits only minority students (Banks 1994). It is true that teaching from a multicultural framework is appealing to minority students (Holland 1992). Students are attracted to an educational approach that provides adequate consideration of the historical contributions and effects of their culture on a profession.

Incorporating a multicultural teaching perspective in the college classroom is, in reality, a benefit to all. Multicultural education enhances multicultural literacy for everyone. Multicultural literacy is linked to people becoming more proficient producers and users of knowledge, participating in world economic life, and enriching their individual lives (Adelman 1992). The goal in teaching from a multicultural perspective is to help students understand society from diverse ethnic and cultural perspectives and to hear the voices of different cultural perspectives. This is one of the primary advantages of having more diverse recreation therapy faculty members: they might be more inclined to teach from a more diverse perspective.

Faculty members in recreation therapy are called upon to organize, plan, develop, and implement strategies and recommend programs and activities for different disability populations. These populations include people with developmental disabilities, physical disabilities, hearing impairments, mental and emotional problems, visual impairments, substance abuse problems, and other issues. They span age groups from infants to geriatrics. Every racial and ethnic group in the United States is represented within each of these populations served through recreation therapy service, yet this racial and ethnic diversification of clients is not proportionally reflected in the overall curriculum, particularly in therapeutic recreation, in U.S. colleges and universities.

In the early developmental stages of recreation therapy, services were based on the concept of assimilation or the metaphor of the melting pot (Peregoy, Schliebner, & Dieser 1997). The concept implied that minority groups could be best served if they took on the characteristics of the majority cultural group in the U.S. As population demographics continue to change and racial and cultural pride takes a more prominent place in the lives of nonwhites, it is evident that the assimilation or melting pot constructs of recreation therapy are inadequate.

For the most part, in therapeutic recreation preparation programs in higher education institutions, the curriculum has been designed to address major issues in services for each of the disability populations mentioned above. In addition, curriculum addresses other essential elements concerning the scope of recreation therapy, such as planning, assessment, evaluation, certification, leisure education, and so on. Although these elements relate to the core of the profession, there may not be adequate consideration of the impact of race, ethnicity, and culture on the delivery of recreation therapy services. More specifically, multicultural issues have been thought to be limited even in many advanced therapeutic recreation educational institutions (Peregoy, Schliebner, & Dieser 1997).

The prevailing curricular view implies that clients/patients should be treated individually — but indifferently with respect to race and culture. At first glance, this curricular view is an acceptable, fashionable, and professionally competent view. However, when providing services to different cultural groups — African Americans and others — not adequately considering the effects of race and ethnicity in recreation therapy planning can have significant consequences and, in fact, may inhibit effective treatment outcomes.

Consequently, race and ethnicity are not well-enough addressed in proportion to the physical, mental, and social problems of clients. As Cornell West (1993) indicated, race continues to matter for many blacks.

In this light, many African Americans perceive that their race is a significant obstacle determining their lot in life. In treatment and rehabilitation, not giving adequate consideration to race may be disrupt the process. In short, recreation therapy services need to take on a broader philosophical view while also addressing more of the current sociopolitical view. This new perspective implies that recreation therapy practice needs to give more attention to particular ethnic perspectives.

An academic and cultural movement is underway in higher education. As the recreation field continues to function within a more diverse U.S. society, issues of race and ethnicity will become increasingly more important in every aspect of the profession. Colleges and universities are being forced to grapple with a continually changing society. These changes present exciting challenges for the recreation therapy and leisure service professions. More and more recreation professionals and practitioners will be expected to work with and have significant knowledge and understanding of people from many cultural, racial, and ethnic backgrounds. While preparing future recreation professionals, recreation educators should ensure that multicultural education perspectives are included in the recreation curriculum.

Butt and Pahonos (1995) found that significant multicultural, racial, and diversity issues are not readily addressed in professional training programs in colleges and universities. In recreation therapy training programs, the situation appears to be the same. In 1995, researchers looked at the inclusion of diversity and multicultural issues in therapeutic recreation master's and doctoral programs in the U.S. (Peregoy & Dieser 1995). The results of this study were interesting: more than half of these training curriculums did not have any type of multicultural program requirement for their students. Some programs indicated that multicultural issues were infused into some courses. Interestingly, it was reported that some programs, at the discretion of the instructor, might address multicultural issues if there was available time. In light of such deficiencies, it has been suggested that colleges, universities, and certifying bodies in the therapeutic recreation field require cross-cultural literacy in their curriculums and professional organizations (Dieser & Wilson 2002).

In higher education, the recreation curriculum has tended to let university "general education" requirements fulfill multicultural education learning. While this practice may be adequate for some professions, the recreation service field needs more profession-specific multicultural education in the core curriculum.

"Multiculturalism springs from the premise that Western civilization in general, and American institutions in particular, are fundamentally racist because they elevate Eurocentric or 'white' standards and values over those of other cultures" (D'Souza 1995, 18). Multicultural education requires that educators instruct future professionals within the context of an entirely new societal balance. Multiculturalism implies that appropriate consideration be given to poverty, native languages, physical and emotional disabilities, and ethnic and racial cultural diversity (Hodgkinson 1988). Conceptually, the multicultural concept is broad (D'Souza 1995) and includes issues such as racism, sexism, and homophobia. While each of these dimensions deserves considerable individual attention, the focus of this book is on ethnic and racial multiculturalism.

In higher education, multiculturalism is often addressed through multicultural education. According to Banks (1994, 81):

> The goal of multicultural education in the broader sense is an education for freedom. First, I mean that multicultural education should help students to develop the knowledge, attitudes, and skills to participate in a democratic and free society. Secondly, multicultural education promotes freedom, abilities, and skills to cross ethnic and cultural boundaries to participate in other cultures and groups. We can empower the Hispanic student to have the freedom to participate in African American culture, and the Jewish student to participate in African American culture — and vice versa. Multicultural education should enable kids to reach beyond their own cultural boundaries.

Multicultural education should not be thought of as a fad. Demographic forecasters have predicted a rapidly growing and diversified population. The 2010 U.S. census data indicates that approximately 39% of the population is nonwhite. Earlier, Pallas, Natriello, and McDill (1989) estimated that by the year 2020, approximately one-half of all students in the U.S. will be people of color. These data indicate a more diverse population. Individuals from various ethnic, racial, and cultural groups will help determine future personal and professional directions in recreation therapy. As a consequence, this more diverse population will demand recreation therapy professionals who are competent and more knowledgeable of cultural differences.

The previous comments imply significant societal and social changes. It is important to note that changing demographic trends often correlate with changes in the university curriculum (Altbach & Lometey 1991). For example, when computers became an efficient method for problem-solving, colleges and universities soon began offering computer-related programs and courses. When certification became a requirement for entry-level recreation therapy practitioners, therapeutic recreation departments took the lead in preparing students for certification, and faculty members helped prepare the therapeutic recreation certification examination. Global and study- abroad program experiences are becoming more routine in higher education, as colleges and universities respond to globalization. In Alabama, a federal judge addressed the question of whether public colleges discriminate against blacks by not offering more multicultural materials in the classroom (Healy 1995). Within this context, universities may be considered more responsible for shaping the cultural and racial perspectives and attitudes of their students.

Colleges and universities are expected to be appropriately sensitive to a multicultural society. As a result, institutions of higher education have begun to pay more attention to diversity and multicultural education, which generally takes place on two tiers: at the university/institutional level and the department/curriculum level. At the university/institutional level, college faculty and administrators might debate how to address multicultural issues. In order to create institutions that are more representative of a multicultural and diverse society, colleges and universities have initiated minority studies programs, created mentoring programs for minority students, created scholarships and awards for minority students, and have attempted to more aggressively recruit and retain minority students and faculty. The idea is that a more diverse university will result in a more sensitive and understanding university community with students better trained for success in a diverse society.

However, much of the attention to multiculturalism occurs at the academic departmental level. Criticism of the traditional university curriculum is not new. "Questions about the purpose, meaning and content of the curriculum trace back to the antebellum debates at Amherst and William and Mary about the classic curriculum, the Yale report of 1828 and its aftermath, the elective system and specialization, and the place of science and the graduate school" (Conrad 1985, 1). However, never before has there been such a debate on the actual content of what is being taught in colleges and universities. With an emphasis on multicultural education, higher education institutions are faced with contradictions in some traditional education foundations. Consequently, multicultural education could be considered a challenge to the traditional higher education curriculum.

Due to the challenge, not everyone is ready to give multiculturalism and multicultural education high marks as an educational or societal priority. Traditionalists argue that writers or scholars who want to add "non-canonical" perspectives to the curriculum are advocating inaccuracies in an ill-fated attempt at inclusiveness. Allan Bloom and Arthur Schlesinger have been two of the most noteworthy critics. Bloom (1987) in his best selling book *The Closing of the American Mind* argues that white American students are not aware of their own culture and that they are ignorant of the philosophical, historical, and economic foundations of the West. Schlesinger (1992), in his popular book *The*

Disuniting of America: Reflections of a Multicultural Society offers one of the more devastating attacks on multiculturalism. He asserts that America is a collection of self-interest groups, celebrating difference while abandoning the idea of assimilation. Schlesinger argues that multiculturalism can be both positive and negative; however, the fragmentation, resegregation, and tribalization it brings are unhealthy for America.

Fisher-Fishkin (1995) offers an interesting response to these traditionalists. She contends that the traditional curriculum is inherently multicultural in nature and that much of the canon has been greatly influenced by nontraditionalists, but this influence needs to be acknowledged and provided fair status.

Nevertheless, current curriculum directives in higher education institutions can take different forms. One of the most utilized curricular patterns in colleges and universities at the undergraduate level is the "interdisciplinary core curriculum" (Gaff 1983). Within this structure, a core curriculum provides a common learning experience for all students. The core curriculum might include courses or specified segments of a course on race, culture, and ethnicity. In this curricular approach, students are expected to get their multicultural education from these general education courses through what might be considered "osmosis" (Adelman 1992). In short, there is an expectation that essentially all cultural information will be, in some way, transposed by students to fit their specific major areas of study.

A major difficulty with the interdisciplinary approach is that it is not discipline specific. Students are more likely to expand their cultural knowledge if multicultural information is included in their specific field of study. The interdisciplinary approach puts discipline-specific cultural information in a secondary position. As Adelman (1992, 32) states, "…the majority of students' academic time is spent acquiring information and skills that are either generic, psychomotor, or devoid of any prima facie cultural and social information…" Therefore, this approach aligns with the proposition that there is not enough discipline-specific diversity education.

While it is true that general education courses can enhance a student's cultural knowledge, a better approach is a course in the student's major study area that addresses cultural information and how it relates to issues in the profession. However, creating new courses that address cultural competence could be met with resistance due to limitations in the total number of degree credit hours, faculty workload restrictions, and accreditation-related requirements for other competence-based and general education courses. Due to these demands, many departments look to the general education area to address their cultural information. The better approach might be the systematic infusion of cultural information throughout a student's discipline-specific coursework. Doyle (2008) was successful in developing such a model, the Integrated Cultural Competence Curriculum (IC-3) Model for Health Education, which could be adapted and modified for therapeutic recreation. In the IC-3 model, cultural competence information is infused throughout the curriculum from introductory courses through the student's internship. The model uses a progressive approach; students build on previously learned cultural information throughout their college studies. The progressive education approach is not new to therapeutic recreation. It is common to require students to master a specific course before taking higher-level, more advanced courses.

Some scholars have stated that a major reason for the ineffectiveness in working with culturally different people is a lack of culturally sensitive material taught in the curriculum (Arrendondo 1985; Ponterotto & Casas 1987; Smith 1982). Success at providing culturally sensitive curriculum material may be closely linked to the active involvement of culturally different faculty members. Ponterotto and Casas (1987) found the most effective culturally sensitive curriculum was developed in institutions when there was a strong commitment by culturally different faculty members, perhaps because minority faculty members may have unique experiences that help stimulate a deeper knowledge and appreciation for issues of minority groups that are affected by economic, social, and educational deprivation.

While teaching is considered a social responsibility (Molnar 1987), some recreation scholars and teachers are encouraging the incorporation of cultural sensitivity within the core recreation curriculum (Aguilar 1990). The basic question for educators becomes, "What should be taught to make the material relevant and render it multiculturally based?"

A curriculum that is multicultural responds to variances in recreation and leisure behavior that are influenced by culture, race, and ethnicity. In addition, a multicultural curriculum is inclusive regarding different cultures, history, and thought. A multicultural curriculum can take form through four approaches: 1) the contributions approach, 2) the additive approach, 3) the transformation approach, and 4) the decision-making social action approach (Banks 1994). The contributions approach is limited and focuses on holidays, heroes, and discrete cultural elements. The additive approach implies that the concepts, themes, and perspectives relating to cultural perspectives are added to the curriculum without changing the curriculum's structure. According to Banks (1994, 26), "Neither the contributions nor the additive approaches challenges the basic structure of the curriculum." The transformation approach requires that the structure of the curriculum be changed to enable students to view concepts, issues, events, and themes from the perspectives of diverse ethnic and cultural groups. In the decision-making social action approach, students make decisions on important social issues and take actions to help solve them (Banks 1994).

These approaches involve teaching courses that focus specifically on race while incorporating experiences based on other diversity areas, including class, gender, sexual orientation, disability, and so forth. These approaches can also involve teaching courses that focus on other discipline-related topics and examine the interplay between race, class, gender, sexual orientation, and the topic area (Ward 1994). The contributions and additive approaches imply inclusion of diverse materials in an effort to ensure that students hear about certain events, while the transformation and social action approaches require more time and effort to accomplish, but are richer in depth. Both approaches require some curriculum adjustment in the recreation therapy classroom. Regardless, teaching multiculturally implies assuring that the various cultural perspectives are incorporated into the curriculum within virtually all courses.

In recreation, reviving the traditional curriculum and making it more multiculturally sensitive will require mainstreaming or inclusion. Many recreation professionals, particularly those in recreation therapy, are familiar with the concepts of mainstreaming and inclusion, which deal with the integration of disabled people with nondisabled people (Kraus & Shank 1992). Mainstreaming implies more integration and less separation of different groups, which can assist all groups in breaking down potential barriers that society imposes with regard to separation. The more that separation occurs, the more likely there will be barriers of understanding between the different groups.

Educators in leisure studies may think of multicultural curriculum integration in the same way that recreation therapy has viewed the values of mainstreaming when working with people who are disabled. By including more relevant multicultural information and perspectives into the core recreation curriculum, students are more likely to develop a better appreciation for diverse cultural perspectives and differences.

For recreation curriculum to address multicultural perspectives more effectively, educators may need to adjust their courses. Ward (1994, 56) writes that educators need to alter curriculum and scholarship that is centered on white Western men to "one that would adequately explain the situations of diverse groups...." This type of curriculum adjustment requires modifications in teaching and course planning. For example, based on Banks's (1994) ideology of the additive approach, educators need to seek additional course materials that enable all students to view the world through different lenses.

Andersen (1988) provides interesting suggestions for educators looking to restructure their courses and mentions ideas such as including more author diversity in course reading; ensuring that race and gender are not segregated in course material; becoming aware of the many situations in which race and gender can be discussed in courses other than poverty and social problems; reframing the ways in which race and gender are addressed with respect to a larger, more dominant culture; and making sure race and gender are seen in their own terms, rather than solely as the dominant group sees them. Embracing these suggestions should help ensure more equality when addressing different racial and ethnic issues in the classroom.

In addition, educators can be effective in the multicultural arena by providing examples of real-life situations of people from different cultural and ethnic groups. For example, while teaching an assessment course, an instructor might first address possible issues in assessing culturally diverse clients and how these issues may be overcome through effective cultural knowledge and establishing the therapeutic trust relationship. Then the educator may discuss and have students identify specific assessment instruments that might be more successful. Finally, the instructor may have students evaluate existing assessment instruments for their most useful and problematic parts in assessing culturally different people.

The previous comments provide examples of what an educator might consider for including multicultural education in assessment. Recreation educators should ensure that culturally relevant information is included not just when a specific topic relating to people from different cultural groups is planned. Rather, this type of information, participation, and discussion should be ongoing in all leisure studies courses.

Students

The underrepresentation of minorities in faculty positions in recreation therapy can also have potential effects on racially or culturally different students considering this profession as a career. One of the major areas of concern for the field of recreation is attracting students of color into academic programs (Bialeschki 1992). For example, Blackwell

(1987) found that black students are more likely to attend colleges and be more satisfied in institutions where more African American faculty members are employed. The findings from Blackwell and other scholars point out that African American students are interested in learning environments that outwardly demonstrate diverse faculties. It is likely that students from different racial groups may feel the same as African American students do; all students may like to see and be taught by faculty who are representative of their own racial or culture group. Subsequently, including a more diverse faculty in recreation therapy may result in additional diverse students enrolling in recreation therapy preparation programs, which in turn will aid in diversity in all levels of the profession.

Minority students currently majoring in recreation therapy may also be affected by the lack of minority faculty in teaching positions. A lack of minority faculty is a serious drawback that may prevent academic and nonacademic supportive relationships between faculty members and minority students. Numerous scholars have emphasized the importance of student-faculty relationships on student development (Astin 1977; Feldman & Newcomb, 1969; Panteges & Creedon, 1978; Katz & Hartnett, 1976). Generally, these scholars have reported the critical impact these involvements have on both minority and majority students. If students are to develop to their best potential, they should have the opportunity for meaningful and substantial relationships with faculty — with both majority and minority faculty members.

For minority students, the student-faculty relationship can be important, especially at the undergraduate level. Some minority students at this level need minority faculty role models, who are crucial for many reasons. First, they symbolize to those students aspiring to teach at the college level that the profession has diversity in its educator sector. Second, these faculty members may inspire those seeking careers in the recreation therapy profession. As a consequence, more students may be influenced to research and study, which will aid in advancing the recreation therapy field with regards to diversity issues.

4. Cultural Competence in Recreational Therapy Practice

Culture is something all people have, whether they realize it or not. We all have ways of being and lessons passed down by previous generations. What we have learned and personally believe has a significant impact on us. These cultural understandings may vary among the perspectives of different racial and ethnic groups. Culture helps individuals organize their lives and feel comfortable in their interactions with others. In order to behave acceptably in a given setting, individuals need to understand and abide by the cultural norms of that setting. Individuals' lives are shaped by various customs, rituals, and taboos. In addition, much of what an individual has learned with respect to these factors helps to serve as the alpha and omega of an individual's existence, not to be questioned.

Even college students have found that cultural differences can impact the relationships they have with their peers, especially foreign students. One study conducted in the United States found that more than one in three foreign students (especially students from China and elsewhere in East Asia) said that they had no college friends, and many wished they had more — and more meaningful — relationships with American students (Fischer 2012, A23). Fischer hypothesized that "cultural differences could be a cause. For example...the United States is a highly individualistic country, while other societies, particularly Asia, put a greater emphasis on social relationships and community ties. These students may be unprepared for Americans' independence and more relaxed attitudes towards friendships...What's more, certain behaviors can be reinforcing...Students from cultures that value deep relationships may find American friendships superficial and choose to associate more with students from their own home country or region."

Professionally, in therapeutic recreation culture plays an important part in shaping the way a recreation therapist thinks, feels, listens, gestures, interprets, and speaks. Everything a person does, thinks, and feels is determined not only by physical heritage or biological nature but also by that individual's reality, context issues, successes, and problems within his or her culture group. Austin (2004) has suggested that recreation therapists often think and act according to their own cultural orientation. A problem with this approach is that professionals may fail to address the cultural mores of those they are working with.

In addition, several terms have been used that address positive interactions between individuals working with people from different racial and ethnic groups, including *culturally sensitive*, *culturally competent*, *culturally effective*, *culturally appropriate*, and *culturally congruent*. Generally, in clinical and non-clinical settings, the terms refer to how healthcare providers and organizations respond effectively to patients' or clients' cultural needs and demonstrate an acknowledgement and acceptance of patients' cultural practices, beliefs, and values. The terms stress the application of appropriate knowledge, skills, and attitudes on the part of the professional in relation to other people's cultures (Goldman, Monroe, & Dube 1996).

To have effective interactions with others from different cultural groups, we need to be culturally competent. This competence is required in many areas, including in sports. The sport of boxing has for years required its referees to communicate effectively with participants. Consider two boxers of equal talent. One speaks English. One speaks Spanish. The referee must be able to communicate effectively with both in order to have a fair boxing match. The referee should provide instructions in English and Spanish to the boxers. The ability to effectively communicate is seen as one of the key components of cultural competence.

No one person can achieve "true" cultural competence, as there are more than 196 countries in the world. Most countries consist of multiple individuals of different races, ethnic groups, religions, social group preferences, languages, traditions, celebrations, attitudes, holidays, education systems, histories, food preferences, governmental structures, opportunities, technologies, and so on. There is simply too much cultural information for one person to dissect and retain. In addition, culture (within groups) incrementally changes over time. For example, if we think back — let's say twenty years ago — and recall our community, schools, religions, technology, and fashions, we'd concede that some aspects of these cultural elements have indeed changed, though foundations of the critical core areas remain constant.

With this in mind, in working towards cultural competence individuals should do as much as they can to learn about the people they are most likely to interact with. People can become more culturally competent if they gain accurate, important, and significant cultural information about an individual and their cultural group

Minorities with Disabilities

As alluded to earlier, cultural competence encourages understanding and thoughtful consideration in three broad areas, including diversity knowledge, historical cultural awareness, and cross-cultural skills. This section will address historical cultural awareness for minorities with disabilities as an example of where recreation therapists can improve care by being more sensitive to issues.

The populations being served by recreational therapy practice have more minority members than population numbers would suggest. The 2010 U.S. census indicates that 12.6% of the U.S. population is African American. A similar percentage could be expected in recreation therapy settings. However, the National Council on Disability found that minorities with disabilities are overrepresented in the disability community. More specifically, the Council reported the following approximate percentages of people with disabilities in each of these populations Native Americans (22%), African Americans (20%), whites (19%), Hispanics (15%), and Asian/Pacific Islanders (10%) (National Council on Disability 1993). Also Walker, (1998) using 1981 U.S. Census data, reported, "There were 22.6 million Americans with significant disability, of which 4.6 million were nonwhite." This equates to about one-sixth of the total disability population. People of minority status are far more likely to have disabilities. Additionally, Bowe (1992) reported there are approximately 2,512,000 African American working-age adults with disabilities in the U.S. Another major prevalence study on minorities with disabilities found that African Americans with disabilities had lower incomes and lower educational levels than their European American counterparts (Asbury et al. 1991). Consequently, research data indicates many people with disabilities in America who are non-white continue to face inequality in the United States. Leaders in minority and disability communities have spoken eloquently about this issue.

> People with disabilities have always been excluded from the bounty of our nation's resources. Minorities with disabilities, in particular, have been the most disenfranchised. It is time that we bring them into the fold as full, first-class participants in our society. — Rev. Jesse Jackson, National Rainbow Coalition (NCD 1993)

> Minority people with disabilities are among the most untapped of our nation's resources. Most have not been given the opportunity to contribute productively to the well-being of our society. It is essential to the success of our country in the 21st Century to utilize the resources of minority people with disabilities. — Larry Brown, Jr., National Council on Disability (NCD 1993)

Some minorities continue to face numerous areas of inequality in America. Some barriers — perceived or real — to equality are either intentional or institutional (Feagin & Feagin 1978). African Americans have been subjected to these barriers since they first arrived in America. Likewise, as the Reverend Jesse Jackson and Larry Brown have stated, people with disabilities also face numerous barriers, as do many minorities. The barriers that the disabled may encounter are often due to a society that has not accommodated their needs. For example, people with disabilities (and some African Americans) continually face discrimination in housing and employment.

Members of minority groups who also have a disability may face a "double bias" of de-valuation or misunderstanding. Both groups have traditionally been and continue to be misunderstood and discriminated against in America. For example, minority group people and people with disabilities have experienced difficulty accessing the healthcare system and benefiting from it. Furthermore, both groups tend to be underrepresented in healthcare personnel, yet the need for minority and disability health and the additional involvement of minority and disability care providers remains important.

Some ethnic people believe that part of the problem is practitioners' cultural insensitivity. Many minority members have had negative experiences with America's healthcare practices. One of the most notable notorious negative healthcare experiences for African American males occurred for forty years, between 1932 and 1972, when the U.S. Public Health Service (PHS) conducted an experiment involving 399 black men in the late stages of syphilis. Most of the men were illiterate sharecroppers in Alabama. The men were never told what disease they had or its seriousness. They were told that they were being treated for "bad blood." Their doctors had no intention of treating them for syphilis. Doctors wanted to use the data collected from the autopsies of the men, so the black men were deliberately left to suffer from the conditions of syphilis, including tumors, heart disease, blindness, insanity, paralysis, and death. The men were deliberately lied to by healthcare professionals. To ensure that the victims would show up for a painful and potentially dangerous spinal tap, the PHS doctors misled them with a letter that indicated this was their last chance for special free treatment. Such behaviors were indicative of some healthcare providers' lack of interest in the well-being of and insensitivity toward blacks. With this type of information circulating in black communities, it is not difficult to understand why blacks are afraid of the services they might receive in America's healthcare system. Many older African Americans passed this information down to younger generations.

The National Council on Disability (NCD), an independent federal agency that works with the president and Congress to increase the inclusion, independence, and empowerment of Americans with disabilities, has made important strides in bringing to light the plight of minorities with disabilities. In 1993, the NCD published the groundbreaking report *Meeting the Unique Needs of Minorities with Disabilities*. This report addressed numerous issues that had been largely overlooked or ignored by U.S. policymakers in the past. It acknowledged that minorities constitute a disproportionate share of the disability community and that they have needs beyond those experienced by other people with disabilities. The 1993 report used the term "double discrimination" to describe this phenomenon in which many minority people with disabilities face discrimination based on both minority status and disability. Significantly, the 1993 report noted that:

- Issues involving minority people with disabilities are complex and require the coordinated attention of many government programs as well as competencies of professionals from many different disciplines.
- As a group, minority people with disabilities are more at risk for health problems, have fewer personal and family resources, have less knowledge and understanding of externally available resources, and fare less well socioeconomically than do minorities without disabilities.
- Staff in service delivery systems, including the state/federal vocational rehabilitation programs, are not sufficiently trained to work with multicultural populations.

- There have been insufficient outreach efforts to include minority people with disabilities in the mainstream of their communities.
- There have been insufficient efforts to address issues concerning the prevention of disabilities that often affect minority people, including racism, violence, substance abuse, and poor general health.
- Education continues to be a key factor for minority people with disabilities in achieving success; therefore, education must be designed to be more positive, focusing on the abilities of children with disabilities rather than on their limitations.
- The Americans with Disabilities Act holds great promise for minority people with disabilities, but the promise will be realized only if specific efforts are made for outreach, education, and removal of barriers in minority communities (National Council on Disability 1993).

In 1999, the NCD published its second significant report on this topic, *Lift Every Voice: Modernizing Disability Politics and Programs to Serve a Diverse Nation*, at a White House forum on disability and cultural diversity. The forum focused on important efforts in how to reduce barriers and improve outcomes in education, employment, and civil rights enforcement for people with disabilities from diverse cultural backgrounds.

Lift Every Voice noted a number of specific barriers that minorities with disabilities face in America including a) barriers to employment, b) barriers to accessing public accommodations, c) barriers to transportation, and d) barriers to culturally competent service delivery. (National Council Disability 1999).

Barriers to culturally competent service delivery represent a rather broad area and include a lack of minority representation within disability service professions, including in positions of decision-making power. Some professionals feel this racial imbalance leads to conflicting expectations and poor communication between service providers and consumers. These are problems that we, as recreation therapists should work to solve within our profession.

Recreational Therapy Personnel

Many healthcare workers, including recreation therapists, come from middle-class backgrounds, bringing with them beliefs representative of their own cultural background and educational training. For example, these practitioners may expect and desire their clients to be open, verbal, and psychologically minded. In addition, in their own training they tend to value verbal, emotional, and behavioral expressiveness and will likely value and expect the same from their clients. They may believe that the development of insight is a sign of a "cure" in a client (Sue 1981). Sensitivity to cultural differences in self-expression, problem solving, and language may not be given adequate attention in the education and training of professional recreation therapists.

Nelson Mandela, the revered South African civil rights leader, alludes to the importance of understanding and acknowledging cultural customs in his international bestselling book *Long Walk to Freedom: The Autobiography of Nelson Mandela*. In the book, Mandela recalls being away from his mother and childhood home for years when he was fighting for the equal rights of black South Africans. On a surprise visit back home to see his mother after years of separation, Mandela writes that when seeing his mother, "We did not hug or kiss; that was not our custom. Although I was happy to be back." (Mandela 1994, 181) As Americans, we might find it difficult to accept such a custom. Yet as many people believe, and eloquently phrased in South Africa's early Freedom Charter when blacks and Indians fought for equal rights, "All people shall have equal rights to use their own language and to develop their own folk culture and customs" (Mandela 1994, 175).

> "...the demand for minority allied health providers is expected to rise...This is good news, considering that this group of practitioners is currently underrepresented in the workforce...precedence must be given to recruit, educate, retain, and graduate minorities today." (Hogan-Hill, et al. 1995, 15).

Although this quote was made many years ago, the implications hold true today: With an increase of culturally different service providers who might be naturally culturally competent in their own particular culture, underserved or inadequately served culturally diverse clients might enjoy more successful or better-understood treatment. The NCD noted that, after a hearing regarding minorities with disabilities, half of the participants testified about the difficulty they had getting culturally competent services due to the lack of minority individuals with disabilities in disability professions (NCD 1993). Further, Juanita Fleming observed that minorities were more underrepresented in healthcare in 1995 than they were fifteen years earlier, and that the need for increased participation of minority healthcare providers was high on the nation's political agenda (Fleming 1995). However, regardless of the ethnic/racial background of the service provider, all clients should be able to receive the best care delivered by culturally competent therapists and practitioners.

A challenge facing recreation therapy and healthcare in general is how to attract and retain recreation therapists with racial and ethnic diversity understanding. This understanding includes the appropriate values, needs, expectations, and languages of consumers. Again, the National Council for Therapeutic Recreation Certification (NCTRC) indicated in 2007 the ethnic background of certified recreation therapists as:

- White (non-Hispanic)   4194   (90.0%)
- Black/African American   263   (5.6%)
- Asian/Pacific Islander   75   (1.6%)
- Hispanic/Latino   74   (1.6%)
- Multi-racial/Multi-ethnic   40   (0.9%)
- Native American/Alaskan Native 7   (0.2%)
- East Indian   6   (0.1%)
- Missing   8

(National Council for Therapeutic Recreation Certification 2007).

Clearly these percentages do not match the current ethnic and racial composition in America. With this limited diversity in the field, it is imperative that practitioners be provided with the necessary training and supervision so their skills can be properly utilized. Such training programs can have an impact on the potential fear, frustration, and embarrassment that may result from language and cultural perception differences.

Recreational therapists have the obligation to ensure that all clients have the opportunity to reach their fullest potential. The client-therapist interactive environment must be conducive to feelings of belonging and personal expression. This relationship should not be based on racial stereotypes or a lack of knowledge regarding individuals of different racial and ethnic groups. Consider the following brief examples and scenarios:

A nineteen-year-old African American male with a recent spinal cord injury who lives in an urban environment enters recreation therapy rehabilitation. The recreation therapist begins the interview portion of the intake process, asking questions only regarding the man's interest in basketball, rap music, and nightlife. Being proficient in sports like basketball, enjoyment of rap music, and a preference for nightlife entertainment are all stereotypes that have been associated with young black males. The client feels a lack of attachment and more distance with the therapist due to this line of questioning. Then the client indicates that he was raised by parents who did not allow him to participate in organized sports, and he feels he is rather uncoordinated physically and never developed an interest in basketball. Later he states he has always had a preference for classical music and seldom goes out to bars and clubs as part of his evening entertainment, preferring to spend his evenings with family, reading, or attending humorous plays. Such a start by the therapist may put a damper on future interactions between the therapist and client.

- - -

A client with Afghan cultural roots wears an *asafetida* bag around her neck during a treatment or rehabilitation session in order to ward off contagious disease. Wearing the asafetida bag, which often contains elements that produce what many people consider to be a pungent smell, might be a common procedure for Afghans as a medical cure. However, to an Afghan patient, the bag may mean a lot psychologically regarding illness prevention. The bag's importance may be that it is a familiar thing in an unfamiliar environment for the client. Should wearing the bag be a major concern to the recreation therapist? It may be more important to realize that the bag is OK as long as it does not hurt the patient.

- - -

Traditional Chinese people may have been taught to believe that personality is derived from blood. With this understanding, an individual may resist blood transfusions. Such beliefs could be significant in developing appropriate and accurate understanding regarding treatments that will be accepted.

- - -

An elderly man of Japanese descent becomes upset and uncooperative because his bed is positioned in a way that, in Japanese culture, is used to display the deceased. This display was disruptive to the gentleman's mental stability, as he was — although probably unintentionally — led to believe that he was doomed to die.

- - -

A Mexican American boy, fifteen years old, is being treated for stage-four cancer on a hospital oncology unit. The boy and his family consistently do not comply with the care treatment team's instructions when he is away from the hospital on Saturdays with his family. When he is home on the visits, the family allows him to eat whatever he wants without regard to his doctor's orders. The family also fails to return the boy on time to the hospital after his home visits. Finally, the family tends to generally disregard the hospital's therapeutic regimen for the boy. These behaviors are thought to be counterproductive to the best client care. However, after subsequent meetings with the boy and his family, they revealed that it was important to them that the family remained central, and that the boy and his family wanted to make the most of their time together. As such, acknowledging the importance of family is an important consideration in this patient's care.

Due to expectations that the United States is the world's leader in many important areas, patients/clients will — and rightfully so — expect recreation therapists to be culturally competent. Regardless of the race of the practitioner, clients will look to recreation therapists as experts and authority figures in their profession. Such professionals need to be knowledgeable about their clients' cultural ways. For many people, sources of authority have traditionally included churches, family, government, schools, and celebrities (Parker 1998). These authority figures will often also include therapists. For clients/patients from different racial and ethnic groups, having someone who understands, sincerely cares for, and instructs them in ways that are sensitive to their cultural group is important to their rehabilitation and treatment.

Yet understanding the world perspective of a person from a different cultural group can represent a significant professional challenge. Some professionals may feel that their education experiences will allow them to completely understand and effectively interact with all members of culturally diverse groups. However, educational programs have tended to focus on pathological lifestyles or maintenance of false stereotypes (Sue & Sue 1990). Various studies have indicated that while national interest in the rehabilitation needs of ethnic groups has expanded during the past decades, the human service profession has failed to meet the particular health needs of these individuals (Bernal & Padilla 1982; Smith 1982). The end result is professionals who deal with issues related to members of minority groups but lack appropriate understanding about cultural and ethnic values. Consequently, many may believe that effective rehabilitation for the culturally different client involves only simple modifications of traditional models of service delivery.

From the beginnings of therapeutic recreation, the general purpose of recreation therapy has been to facilitate the development, maintenance, and expression of an appropriate leisure lifestyle (Peterson & Gunn 1984). Within this conceptual definition is the assumption that recreation therapy can aid in developing personally rewarding leisure functioning and encourage changes in the clients served, with the primary goal of an independent leisure lifestyle. This conceptual philosophy of therapeutic recreation continues to be held by many recreation therapy practitioners. Consequently, therapeutic recreation is thought to be concerned with allowing people with varying disabilities to obtain an appropriate social, recreation, and leisure lifestyle.

Within this conceptualization of recreation therapy, the underlying proposition assumes that recreation therapy involves a process. Peterson and Gunn (1984) further maintain the use of therapeutic recreation activities as a well-planned process that involves a) assessing the client's functional problem, b) planning treatment goals, c) selecting appropriate activities, and d) selecting an appropriate interaction and intervention style.

Finally, Vawter and others (2003) recommend that in order for healthcare practitioners to provide culturally sensitive healthcare, they need to:

- Be aware of the influence of culture on health status, beliefs, practices, and values (appreciating that culture influences an individual's health status and practices)

- Increase self-awareness about their own health beliefs, practices, and values (reflecting on their own beliefs, practices, and values, and how they may have evolved)
- Learn about prevailing health beliefs, practices, and values of the cultural group they serve (making efforts to learn about a cultural group's social, economic, and political situation, healthcare status, access to healthcare, and possible health disparities)
- Identify potential areas of congruity and difference between their own health beliefs, practices, and values and those of the cultural groups they serve (being alert to possible areas of miscommunication and misunderstanding that can arise due to differences between beliefs about causes, cures, and so on)
- Increase self-awareness about their own cross-cultural health care ethics (when faced with differing or alternative cultural perspectives, learning more about them, accommodating them, and adapting to them)
- Learn skills to identify, evaluate, and respond to cross-cultural ethical conflicts, with special attention to challenges to professional integrity (dealing with cultural values or practices that may conflict with professional integrity of the practitioner)
- Develop attitudes culturally responsive to the groups they serve (displaying attitudes and behaviors that are respectful of the groups they work with)
- Learn communication skills culturally responsive to the groups they serve (being mindful that greetings, eye contact, hand gestures, voice tone, amount of touch allowed, and facial expressions may vary in interpretation for each cultural group)
- Develop skills in applying culturally responsive knowledge, skills, and attitudes to particular clinical encounters (being willing to listen, explain, acknowledge similarities and differences, recommend courses of action, negotiate, and evaluate cross-cultural conflicts and responses)

Marginality and Ethnicity

In order to assist with and provide recreation therapy for African Americans and people in other minority groups, recreation therapists should have at least a rudimentary understanding of the scholarly research of minority group recreation participation and involvement. This section provides an overview of some of the basic research on recreation participation, primarily of African Americans.

The recreation and leisure participation patterns of individuals from different racial and ethnic groups can be complex. Educators, researchers, and recreation professionals have been concerned with patterns and issues regarding the recreational and leisure behavior of minority groups since the 1960s (Mueller & Gurin 1962; Washburne 1978; McDonald & Hutchison 1987; Floyd & Gramann 1993; Floyd et. al. 1994). Included within these efforts has been the desire to determine if there are differences in leisure and recreational behavior based on racial/cultural differences of individuals (Holland 2002).

The majority of the research on the recreation preferences, leisure experiences, and participation patterns of minority groups, particularly African Americans, has been on outdoor recreation pursuits and urban areas (Floyd & Gramann 1993; McDonald & Hutchison 1987). Generally, studies have been limited to the participation patterns of minority group members in these selected areas. For example, Carr and Williams (1993) found that Hispanic immigrants with high levels of acculturation were more likely to indicate escaping the city as the primary reason for visiting outdoor recreation facilities. Similarly, Floyd and Gramann (1993) indicated that acculturation and primary structural assimilation affected Mexican American participation in recreation. Furthermore, some scholars suggest that a lack of participation in recreation and leisure activities is related to a lack of interest by that population. However, other evidence suggests that many minority group members may underutilize certain programs and activities due to cultural insensitivity within the programs themselves, in addition to service providers' attitudes and misperceptions.

More specifically, research regarding recreation participation preferences and patterns comparing blacks and whites has indicated some differences. The results have been largely attributed to the income level or the residential areas of the study participants. For example, in an early study Cheek, Field, and Burdge (1976) found few leisure and recreational differences between groups when income levels and residential areas were similar between groups. Also, Washburne (1978) found differences between blacks and whites relating to wildlife recreational participation. In general, research indicates that whites participated more often in wildlife recreation activities than blacks did. Furthermore, Kornegay and Warren (1969) reported that African Americans' preference for specific outdoor recreational activities differs from that of whites, while proposing that if we look at preferences for activities rather than activities actually engaged in, black and white differences may increase rather than decrease.

Hauser (1962) observed that the greater the degree of urbanization for both groups, the greater the likelihood of similar recreation participation between blacks and whites. Kornegay and Warren (1969) found vacation travel was less frequent and involved shorter distances in black households than in white households. O'Learly and Benjamin (1981) found that for many recreational activities, blacks were more likely than whites to use city or town recreational resources rather than rural resources; blacks were more likely to participate in activities closer to their homes. The differences and inconsistencies regarding recreational and leisure patterns of blacks indicates that we know relatively little about blacks and recreation and leisure (Dwyer & Hutchison 1990).

The reasons for differences in recreation and leisure interest and participation have been debated in the leisure profession. Two different theories dominate the literature: the marginality theory and the ethnicity theory (Hutchison 1988; McDonald & Hutchison 1987; Hutchison & Fidel 1984; Wendling 1981; Washburne 1978; Floyd et. al. 1994). According to McDonald and Hutchison (1987, 28), "The socioeconomic-demographic [marginality] theory is based upon the notion that individuals with similar socioeconomic status will be more likely to participate in similar outdoor recreation activities. Subsequently, variations in outdoor recreation behavior may be a function of social class, as opposed to race." The marginality theory relies on the notion that black and white differences in recreation participation are due to the collective lower socioeconomic position of blacks in society. This theory aligns with an assumption that more similarity in participation and interest will occur if socioeconomic differences, which may be related to differences in opportunities, are eliminated. Opportunities relate to the availability and accessibility of programs and facilities.

The success of some minority athletes in what have been traditionally considered "white sports" aligns with the marginality theory. Examples include Tiger Woods in golf; Debi Thomas, Olympic ice skater; Venus and Serena Williams in tennis; Dominique Dawes, John Orozo, and Gabby Douglas, Olympic gymnasts; and Cullen Jones, Olympic freestyle sprint swimmer. That many of these athletes have advocated for and started foundations and organizations aimed toward increasing minority participation in their sports may be considered an opposing argument to the following theory, ethnicity theory.

In contrast, the ethnicity theory proposes that black and white differences in recreation interest and participation are due to distinctive differences relating to an individual's subculture. Ethnicity refers to the cultural characteristics of a minority group. This theory calls for an acknowledgement of the inherent differences between each ethnic group, wherein recreational professionals should provide leisure opportunities that are in line with the interest of each group. In a nutshell, the ethnicity theory asserts that blacks and whites tend to engage in specific recreation pursuits due to membership in their particular ethnic groups.

The previous theories indicate it is theoretically problematic to attribute any one single reason for blacks' — or any other racial group's — leisure patterns. Philipp (1993, 292) offered four reasons for these difficulties: "(1) it is highly difficult to briefly characterize an entire race in a large, diverse, and highly mobile country like America; (2) the long history of discrimination and segregation against blacks has produced a heightened sense of group consciousness and a stronger orientation toward collective values and behavior than exist generally among Americans, and group consciousness remains strong among blacks today producing a unique black identity; (3) the functional and behavioral effects of this institutionalized prejudice and discrimination are difficult to measure, and even more difficult to address via public and private initiatives; and (4) there remains so little empirical evidence in the literature upon which to convincingly base theoretical arguments."

Adhering to either theory can be problematic due to several factors that may influence recreation participation. As an example, the health benefits of physical activity and exercise are becoming common knowledge. Yet when compared to whites, blacks are believed to exercise less. When comparing black and white avid recreational runners, it was believed that lack of role models, unsafe community streets, and social pressure from other blacks could be important influences on African Americans (Jennings 2011).

Again, the dominant theories that account for differences primarily relate to participation and involvement in the outdoor recreation area. Recently, the National Outdoor Leadership School (NOLS) initiated a program that acknowledges the limited involvement by minority youth — specifically African American youth — in outdoor nature activities. The NOLS is programming the first African American expedition to Denali, the highest peak in North America. Further, the NOLS intends to increase role models in communities traditionally underrepresented in the outdoors. The initiative was set for summer 2013, just as this book was being finalized (National Outdoor Leadership School 2012). However, professionals in recreation therapy are not only involved in programming in the outdoor recreation area, they must also understand factors that may impact leisure participation and interest in other aspects in the lives of the minority clients they serve, such as leisure awareness, leisure lifestyle, self-concept, and life satisfaction.

The previous findings indicate that recreational professionals, including recreation therapists, may not know enough about the recreation and leisure patterns of African Americans or other minority group members and, as a consequence, may not know what approaches to take when programming for members of these groups.

In recreation therapy, in order to develop, plan, and execute the most effective client rehabilitation and community re-entry program, recreation therapists must understand potential differences in leisure activity patterns. There's little research in the therapeutic recreation profession literature regarding minority group leisure activity, participant interest, and participation. Recreation therapy scholars and practitioners will need to investigate potential factors that may impact the recreation and leisure participation of the racial and ethnic groups that they are interested in or work with. They must also work carefully with individual clients by being aware of possible issues arising from ethnic differences.

Culturally Competent Assessment

Skills in the initial interaction of client assessment set the tone and potential success for the rest of the therapeutic recreation process. Decisions during the assessment process affect target areas, treatment, and determinations for the rest of the treatment and rehabilitation. Important in the assessment process is determining specific instruments used to solicit information regarding a client and to make analytical assumptions after observing or interacting with a client.

For example, a researcher experienced a situation in which a young child had recently moved with his family from Samoa to the U.S. During an assessment of early motor functioning, the child was observed as clumsy with delayed motor development. Later the child was observed at his parents' home, where he moved freely with limited to no difficulty. Researchers determined that the Samoan home was furnished like a traditional Samoan home with mats and low furniture, with none of the larger obstacles common to American homes. The child had never been exposed to nor had the opportunity to move about in different environments (Lynch & Hanson 1997). With a better understanding of traditional Samoan household structures, the initial assessor may have been able to more accurately assess the child's developmental status.

Assessment is when recreation therapists collect relevant data regarding patient/client history. The basic premise of addressing cultural information during the assessment process is that patients/clients have a right to maintain their cultural values, beliefs, and practices, and these factors should be considered, respected, and understood while patients/clients are in the therapist's care (Leininger 1978).

Assessment instruments, critical to the assessment process, determine where along a continuum an individual fits regarding a specific criteria. The nature of cultural differences of individuals from ethnic groups in America warrants attention in this continuum. African Americans, Latinos, and Native Americans as a group have not performed as well as whites on formal tests and assessments. Data from several studies and national assessments consistently confirm this (Applebee, Langer, & Mullis 1987; Educational Testing Service 1988; National Center for Education Statistics 1988). Much of the data reveals that the most important factors accounting for assessment differences between whites and culturally different groups relate to poverty and English language proficiency.

Are other factors related to differences in assessment or test results? In general, the literature indicates that differences between whites and other groups are significantly reduced when comparisons are limited to individuals with similar income levels and similar English proficiency. Nevertheless, some of the early variance can be explained due to the roots of discrimination in test development. For example, in 1916 the Stanford-Binet Intelligence Test was developed in France and later translated into English to reflect American values and knowledge. The test was normed on middle-class white children (Mercer 1989). When girls outscored boys on the test, the test designers, with an assumption that girls could not be more intelligent than boys, concluded the test had serious flaws. In 1937, the developers revised the test and eliminated the items in which the girls outperformed the boys, while at the same time not eliminating or revising the items that favored urban over rural children or children of professional fathers over day laborers (Mercer 1989). Consequently, it appears that the cultural differences apparently matched the test developers' expectations of how intelligence and achievement should be distributed across groups. So what was supposedly an era of objective and efficient testing and assessment actually historically shows some degrees of racism, classism, and sexism in many early instruments (Chachkin 1989; Mercer 1989). In short, the original developers of some assessment instruments, particularly those measuring intelligence and aptitude, apparently were not concerned about test or assessment bias because they believed it was possible to assess intelligence independently of environment. When assessing many members of cultural groups, it is critical that environmental factors affecting assessment results be adequately addressed.

Sue and Sue (1990) indicated that personality tests that reveal African Americans as being suspicious, mistrustful, and paranoid need to be understood from a larger social-political perspective. The therapist who puts complete trust in traditional paper assessment results may obtain only a partial picture of the African American client. Therapists must be cognizant that, historically, many forms of assessment and evaluation were based on white and middle class perspectives. While using a traditionalistic perspective, a therapist who finds a client mistrustful, suspicious, and paranoid may not be able to accurately understand potential reasons for such findings. Adhering to the traditionalistic perspective enhances bias in diagnosis and treatment. Considering that many African Americans continue to be victims of prejudice and discrimination, we might reasonably expect mistrust, suspicion, and paranoia.

Even when recreation therapists have little direct experience with African Americans, simply being employed as "helping" professionals may lead to the assumption that they have no prejudice, bias, or discomfort that may interfere with their work. It may be more truthful that although overt prejudice may be absent, practitioner discomfort or inexperience may be reflected in the benign neglect of an issue. Due to a lack of knowledge and understanding, staff may direct efforts in leisure and recreational activities incorrectly. Neglect of racial or cultural issues may impede the client's progress. Consequently, the African American client may be urged or pushed toward leisure pursuits that have little in common with their cultural perspective. When this occurs, in some instances clients may feel uncomfortable revealing their true feelings to the therapist — they may have been taught that therapists are "experts." Rather than indicating their true feelings, some clients/patients may simply go along with what a therapist prescribes.

It is easy to see that the recreation therapist plays an integral role in the assessment of all clients, including culturally different clients. Not only is it important which assessment instrument is used, but the therapist's understanding and sensitivity regarding the client and the client's leisure and life experiences are also critically important. If the recreation therapist is to obtain accurate, reliable, and valid assessment results in a way that is most useful, potential uncertainties that may affect assessment interpretation must be effectively addressed.

Recreation therapists who conduct assessments on clients representing different cultural groups may find it difficult to choose assessment instruments that provide appropriate insights to adequately address cultural differences. Instruments should be selected with care, because developmental norms and expectations may differ from group to group.

Individuals from different racial or cultural groups who have little or no cognitive dysfunction are the clients most likely to understand bias and discrimination, and as a consequence, they are more likely to harbor differing, negative, and defensive attitudes and behaviors towards some individuals in the mainstream. Consequently, before beginning the assessment process, it is important to consider the psychological, sociological, and developmental level at which the client is functioning.

It's likely in client assessment that the recreation therapist needs the most significant degree of cultural competence. A basic tenet of assessment is gathering information on clients in order to improve the quality of their lives. In achieving this goal, recreation therapy practitioners should seriously consider the individual's culture as an important determinant in problem identification and problem resolution, which are integral components of the assessment process. The capability of the practitioner to adequately focus on cultural elements includes

- the ability to be comfortable with differences in others;
- the ability to control or change false beliefs;
- the ability to respect and appreciate the values, beliefs, and practices of people who are culturally different;
- the ability to understand that there are multiple ways of thinking and behaving;
- the ability to behave flexibly (Pinderhughes 1989).

What happens when a client's or patient's value system is in conflict with the therapist's cultural underpinnings? Ineffective assessment, treatment, and discharge planning is likely to occur. While some scholars, writers, and practitioners have given more attention to assessment instruments in recreation therapy, much less has been written about assessment for culturally different groups.

Assessment instruments and assessment information may be objective or subjective. Both types of data on clients from other cultures can be misunderstood and misinterpreted if the practitioner has not had sufficient experience or enough exposure to recreational and social activities as they relate to other cultures.

Subjective data — data obtained directly from the client — is critical in the assessment stage. This data can be misinterpreted if the practitioner is not adept at picking up on crucial cues and clues the client may provide. Jargon or cultural and ethnic peculiarities by members of racial and ethnic groups can sometimes be misunderstood and misinterpreted by members of other cultures. For example, Peregoy and

Dieser (1997) made this point nicely when they observed that therapists incorrectly assessed their Native American clients' lack of direct eye contact as an indication of low self-esteem, while in reality avoiding eye contact in Native American culture can be an indicator of respect.

Objective data — data obtained from sources other than the client — also requires practitioner knowledge and sensitivity to cultural differences. Particularly when the client's recreational, leisure, social, environmental, and economic factors are assessed, it is crucial that the practitioner essentially enter the client's world to get the best picture of the client's situation. Only then can the practitioner provide the most productive assessment and subsequent treatment and rehabilitation for the client.

The client assessment process has several parts, each requiring recreation therapist proficiency. As the number of assessment instruments used by recreation therapists continues to grow, many therapists may feel relatively comfortable administering and utilizing them. Nevertheless, one area of the assessment process involves generating target areas for clients based on these assessment results. This is the area where recreation therapists may feel uncomfortable when assessing people from different cultural groups (McCabe & Malkin 1999). In addition, Stumbo (2001, 221) stated, "It is not surprising that therapeutic recreation specialists often enter their jobs with less than adequate competence and continue to experience difficulties in the client assessment process throughout their careers." McCabe and Malkin (1999) found moderate to high demand for training in the following areas: 1) assessment of individuals from differing cultural groups, 2) making diagnostic decisions regarding clients from different cultural groups, and 3) training in formal and informal assessment strategies for individuals from different cultural groups. Interestingly, many of the study's respondents indicated that they understood the issues of potential bias regarding particular assessment tools. Much of the bias may be due to the nature and development of assessment instruments used in professional recreation therapy practice.

Generally, there are two different types of assessment instruments: norm-referenced (standardized assessment instruments which have been subjected to the rigors of validity and reliability) and criterion-referenced (often developed by therapists for specific agencies, or basing analysis on informal interactions with clients). Norm-referenced assessments have results that can be compared against a larger sample population, while criterion-referenced assessments are based on achievement of skills based on hierarchical functioning (Peterson & Gunn 1984). Stumbo (1991) has suggested one of the problem areas in recreation therapy is a general lack of assessment instruments that are reliable and valid. One of the main difficulties with the process of norming assessments is that the process itself leans toward the mainstream culture (Garcia & Pearson 1994). When this occurs, small numbers of people from different cultural groups are likely to be included in research study sample participants. In other words, there is racial and cultural underrepresentation in the sample. When underrepresentation occurs, the sample may have a certain degree of content bias. Content bias occurs when assessment content and procedures reflect "the dominant culture's standards of language function and shared knowledge and behavior" (Garcia & Pearson 1994, 335). Padilla (1979) and Trokie (1984) found that content bias was most severe when assessment tasks, topics, and vocabulary reflect the culture of the mainstream society to such an extent that it is difficult to do well on formal assessments without being culturally assimilated. In short, the literature alludes to an assertion of shortcomings in the assessment development arena. Many of the pitfalls can be reduced by looking more closely at the role of the recreation therapists in the assessment process.

Finally, client assessment is a critically important professional responsibility. Assessment is the primary method for establishing an accurate baseline of a client's recreational and leisure preferences, interests, limitations, potentials, and knowledge. Recreation therapists who need to write effective treatment plans realize how important efficient assessment is to the individual treatment process. Yet client assessment can be problematic. Stumbo (1991) provides a general summary of many problems associated with client assessment, including a) lack of assessment tools; b) limited scope, content, and intent; c) lack of psychometric adequacy; d) lack of specialist expertise; and e) lack of availability. More specifically, Stumbo (2001) further asserted a paucity of appropriate and standardized assessment instruments in addition to a lack of available information regarding culturally different clients. Assessing clients in recreation therapy would be simple if all clients were similar. However, this is not the case. In fact, recreation therapists are taught that all clients are individuals and should be treated that way. In the assessment arena, however, the "one size fits all" approach may be the one most often applied.

In conclusion, in client assessment in therapeutic recreation, leisure patterns and behaviors cannot be considered separate from the broader context of a person's life and lifestyle. In fact, the broader context of the culturally different person's lifestyle must be given significant attention during the assessment process. The culturally different individual may face different societal realities which may have an impact on their life's perceptions — which in turn affects recreation and leisure participation opportunities, interest, motivation, and access. In general, culturally different people may be more likely to be affected by poverty, racial prejudice, bias, and so on. These realities need to be given significant attention during the assessment and treatment planning process in recreation therapy.

Self-Appraisal

Before the actual client assessment process commences, some specific personal and professional issues need to be addressed. "Health care professionals must be sensitive not just to others' personal cultural beliefs, practices, and values, but also their own belief systems. This self-assessment is critical to successfully negotiating a culturally competent, treatment plans for African Americans" (McNeil 2002, 27). In self-assessment, recreation therapists might partake in a self-evaluation process and conduct a serious exploration of their own cultural background, examining their own potential prejudices and biases as they relate to other cultures (Campinha-Bacote 1998). This process involves a critical appraisal of personal and professional issues relating to race, culture, and the appropriateness of leisure interest pursuits. The self-appraisal need not take place at the start of every client assessment. Rather, after the self-appraisal, it should be reviewed continually as a habit of mind.

With respect to the self-appraisal, at the outset the terms "minority" and "underrepresented group member" could be addressed. These terms are often used when referring to culturally different people. Both terms are suspect. The term *minority* carries with it a rather negative connotation; we tend to think a minority is something less than something else. Some organizations and individuals overuse the term, using it whenever they refer to any person who is not white. Although the term as defined in Webster's Dictionary means "the smaller number of two groups representing the whole," in reality, the majority of people in the U.S. relate it to being something other than white. The term *underrepresented* may be more suitable when referring to someone who is not white. Underrepresentation as used in today's context often describes groups who have been traditionally excluded in opportunities, access, rights, privileges, and so forth by a white-male-dominated society. Included within this group are people representing ethnic and cultural groups, women, people with disabilities, and others. Addressing such issues with appropriate terminology when referring to people who are racially or culturally different from the majority culture could be a beginning to the self-appraisal.

Are there other issues that might assist with self-appraisal? Recreation therapists might want to address such questions as:

- What kinds of leisure activities, experiences, and attitudes are particular to different cultures?
- What factors might affect the leisure motivation and interest of culturally different clients?

- How do I (the recreation therapist) feel about culturally different individuals whose leisure lifestyle is in opposition to what I feel is a holistically effective, leisure-focused individual?
- How much do I really know about culturally different experiences (leisure or otherwise)?
- If a culturally different person appears to have a negative attitude toward recreation therapists or certain prescribed leisure activities, is the individual justified in harboring negative feelings/attitudes?
- If I am to function at the most effective level in a future America, which of the following viewpoints must I adopt? a) Majority conformity, b) Melting pot, c) Pluralist, d) Separatist.

A self-appraisal such as this likely will affect the self-awareness of the recreation therapist. This type of self-appraisal is a very important aspect of the assessment process, particularly when assessing members of different cultural groups. In the self-appraisal, the recreation therapist seeks empathy for and understanding of themselves and of people who are culturally different. Empathy within this context is the ability of professionals to effectively put themselves in the place of the culturally different clients, aspiring to see the world from each client's perspective. On the surface, empathy appears to be a simple process of role reversal. Yet empathy is not easy. Empathy can be risky. In order to effectively empathize with someone from a different culture or race, we have to be open, highly evaluative, and critical of our own cultural perspectives. To be highly critical of our own culture requires courage. The professional must question many of the beliefs and understandings they have been reared with and have taken for granted — and which have been embedded in and through our society's traditions. The self-appraisal can be a personally perilous endeavor.

These additional questions can be used as an aid for the recreation therapist during the self-appraisal process.

- Have I earnestly sought out information to enhance my own awareness and understanding of stereotypes, racism, bias, and prejudice (talking to others, reading, listening)?
- Have I spent time recently looking at my own attitudes and behaviors as they contribute to or combat stereotypes, racism, bias, and prejudice around and within me?
- Have I reevaluated my use of terms, phrases, or behaviors that may be perceived by others as being degrading or hurtful?
- Have I openly confronted a racist joke, comment, or action among those around me?
- Have I made a personal commitment within myself to stand against racism and prejudice? Have I considered the risk of such a stand?
- Have I become increasingly aware of potential stereotypical, racist, or prejudiced programming in advertising, slogans, and textbooks?
- Have I implemented discussions aimed at understanding and eliminating discrimination, bias, or stereotypical behavior?
- Have I become seriously dissatisfied with my own level of activity in combating racism, sexism, ageism?
- Have I contributed time or funds to an agency, fund, or program that actively confronts intolerance and racism?
- Have I ended affiliations with organizations which are racist, sexist, and so on?
- Have I subscribed to a publication that will educate me in a culture other than my own?
- Have I made an effort to learn some of the language of those in my community or facility who may speak something other than standard English?

Through addressing such questions as these, the recreation therapist can develop a better understanding of themselves and racial or cultural diversity.

Informal Interaction

Once the recreation therapist completes a self-appraisal and understands the diversity of the leisure experience, the therapist is ready to begin the assessment. However, before the actual assessment begins, the recreation therapist and the client usually have an informal initial face-to-face interaction. This is a time when important first impressions — and sometimes lasting impressions — are established. A primary purpose of this interaction should be developing an understanding relationship between the client and the therapist.

The recreation therapist should understand that the accuracy of the assessment depends upon the accuracy of the information obtained. This makes the initial meeting for the therapist and the patient/client crucial: effective communication and rapport should be established prior to the actual assessment.

Campinaha-Bacote (1998) maintains that three or four interactions with individuals of different cultural groups can sometimes provide a knowledge base about that particular cultural group. However, three or four patients' values, practices, and beliefs may or may not be representative of all members of that particular group. Consequently, many encounters may be needed to effectively understand and interact with the group.

There is no recommended time frame in which this interaction is to take place. For some clients, only a few minutes are necessary. For other clients, the time needed during this interaction phase may be much greater. The therapist should be flexible and realize that clients from some cultural group may be suspicious and distrustful of the therapist and what the assessment information will be used for. At this time it is important to be honest and gain the trust of the client.

The informal interaction helps bridge a potential gap between the therapist and the client. The potential gap is not a personalized declaration by either the therapist or the client. Rather it may have been caused by a history of misunderstanding or discrimination. The informal interaction phase should not be taken for granted. Gaining the confidence and trust of an individual who may have different perceptions, feelings, and experiences than those of the recreation therapist may take time. It is a rather precarious situation, because it is the therapist who is essentially being evaluated. Imagine that! Roles may be reversed for a short while. In this role reversal, the client assesses the therapist by whatever means that they have to determine if this is a person to be trusted or a person who maintains a prejudice towards culturally different people.

The informal interaction may begin by demonstrating sensitivity to the patient's/client's needs by explaining the recreation therapist's role in treatment. Initially, the therapist should ask the patient/client how they would like to be addressed (the client's name listed on the chart may not be their preferred name). Some individuals have professions (Dr., Reverend) or roles (Mr., Mrs.) or names or titles that they prefer. Although rather basic, this beginning courtesy may go a long way in establishing a positive relationship with a patient/client.

During the informal interaction, it is important to establish common ground through sharing experiences and exchange of information. The therapist should demonstrate a caring approach by being considerate and polite while giving the appearance of being unhurried. Finally, during this encounter, the therapist should not be afraid to ask about something that they are unfamiliar with or unsure about. Honest questioning and dialogue can be interpreted as showing interest in the patient/client, respect for their culture, and a willingness to learn and understand.

Finally, it is critically important for the recreation therapist to listen to their clients during this process. Some early scholars have suggested that recreation therapists have not always taken the time to appropriately listen and understand individuals from different cultures (Sylvester, Voelkl, & Ellis 2001).

Assessment Interviews

An interview may be used as an effective assessment method for virtually all clients. Due to a lack of reliable and valid standardized assessment instruments, recreation therapists will often have to obtain client information from talking with their clients (Ferguson 1989). The assessment interview is a one-to-one conversational interaction between the recreation therapist and the client.

Although the interview may be considered one of the least reliable methods for gathering assessment information, with a culturally different client it may be one of the most effective for obtaining relevant cultural information. Considering that the therapist must understand the world of the client, very few — if any — standardized methodologies allow such flexibility in gathering this difficult to obtain and potentially complex information. Realizing the individualistic and personal nature of the leisure experience, we might wonder if any other methods are more reliable, valid, and suitable to elicit the needed information. Recognizing potential differences regarding leisure experiences related to race, income, culture, age, experiences, opportunity, skills, prejudice, and so on, the recreation therapist seeks to answer not only a client's recreational and leisure skills and preferences but also why they do what they do (Fain & Shank 1989).

The purpose of the interview as an assessment tool is to obtain data regarding the client's recreational and leisure pursuits, values, interest, and motivation (Ferguson 1989). The interview can be a powerful technique, allowing the recreation therapist an avenue for detailed information relative to the client's leisure experience. However, it's not only the interview questions themselves that allow the gathering of the most useful data — it's also the therapist who administers and guides the process that makes for the most effective interview. Selecting the correct assessment tool is important. Equally important are therapist-patient interaction factors, such as voice tone, eye contact, body language, facial expressions, and so on. In addition, it is important that the therapist listens with interest and respect and remains nonjudgmental about the information solicited.

In conclusion, after completing the self-appraisal and the informal interaction, the recreation therapist should be prepared to guide the client through the interview. The following sample is a list of questions intended to solicit cultural information from patients/clients. Reasons for asking the questions are in italics.

Interview Guide

1. What do you do in your free time? What recreation and leisure activities do you currently participate in?

    The recreation therapist needs to identify the current recreational and leisure participation pattern of the client.

2. What kinds of recreational and leisure activities are prevalent in your community?

    By identifying the types of recreational and leisure activities in the patient's community, the therapist can make more informed decisions regarding the type of environment to which the client is likely to return. It makes little sense to develop a treatment plan based solely on the materials and facilities available to the recreation therapist. Where the client is going upon return to their community, and the opportunities and challenges there, should also be considered.

3. What kinds of recreation and leisure activities have you previously participated in?

    The recreation therapist seeks an understanding of past participation of the client. This is essential in understanding the types of opportunities available to the client in the past. If a person has had little or no access to particular experiences, it may not benefit the client if the therapist makes judgments based on a hypothetical view of what a holistic leisure lifestyle entails.

4. Why did you participate in these activities?

    The recreation therapist seeks understanding of the motivation that led to participation in past leisure pursuits.

5. If you stopped participating in these activities, when did that happen and why did you stop?

   The recreation therapist seeks to understand the reasons for discontinuation of specific leisure pursuits.

6. What other kinds or types of recreation and leisure activities would you like to participate in?

   The therapist needs to determine the client's knowledge base of activities. If a client's knowledge is limited, the therapist may want to broaden it.

7. What prevents you from participating in these other activities?

   After successfully increasing the client's knowledge base, the therapist seeks a general understanding of the client's perceptions of barriers that may limit involvement in different activities.

8. Do you feel that your race and/or culture have an impact on your present leisure pursuits?

   The recreation therapist seeks specific understanding of the perceived impact of race and/or culture on the client's leisure participation.

9. Do you feel that you are free to participate in any recreational or leisure activity that you wish? Why? Why not?

   Determining the specific kinds of recreational and leisure pursuits in which the client would like to participate provides a starting point in understanding the perception of barriers that inhibit certain leisure participation. In addition, the therapist seeks information regarding the client's perception of their race and its relationship to recreation and leisure involvement.

10. Do you normally participate in leisure activities alone or with others? Explain.

Determining recreational/leisure participation patterns will aid the therapist in determining the type of programming most suitable for the client. This information is especially useful in the early stages of treatment. Determining the readiness level of the client regarding involvement with group sizes can affect the long-term treatment of the client.

11. With whom do you enjoy participating in recreational and leisure activities? Why?

12. Do you engage in recreation and leisure activities with individuals from other races or cultural groups? Explain.

    It is important to understand and preferences or prejudices the client may have regarding other racial or ethnic groups.

13. Is recreation and leisure involvement important to you? Why? Why not?

    The therapist seeks to determine how the client views recreation and leisure involvement. Recreation/leisure values may be related to specific race and cultural variables. For example, some racial and cultural groups may perceive recreational and leisure involvement as less important than work. Reliable and valid instruments are available if the therapist needs more detailed information (burlingame and Blaschko 2010).

14. Do you feel that what you do or how you behave during a recreational or leisure activity pursuit is perceived by others as being representative of your race? Sometimes? Never? Always?

15. Do you feel that you and your racial group are treated fairly by the general public? Explain.

    The previous two questions specifically address feelings, attitudes, and perceptions about race, bias, and prejudice, which are important for evaluating the client's cultural competence and helping the therapist achieve cultural competence.

After an interview such as this, the recreation therapist may have a better understanding of the culturally different client and their understanding of the impact of race and culture on the leisure experience.

5. Conclusions

Recreation therapists need to be good diagnosticians to best serve clients; they must accurately diagnose what is going on in the client's leisure life and community in order to plan an effective treatment program. A more diverse society will have a direct impact upon the recreation field and how professionals should be trained. For many recreation professionals currently working in larger metropolitan areas, changing demographics are a reality. In many cities, a majority of residents represent various racial and ethnic groups. To work more effectively with these diverse groups, recreation professionals need to develop a better understanding of different cultural groups and recognize the ethnic and cultural differences that may affect recreation and leisure interest, motivation, participation, and outcomes.

This cultural change means that recreation professionals can no longer assume that most people they work with look, sound, and see the world as they do. Cultural differences may make it more difficult to establish and maintain relationships with potential clients if the recreation therapist is not culturally competent. How well the recreation professional adjusts and adequately deals with these realities will affect professional cultural competence.

As U.S. society becomes more diverse, the recreation field will need to find ways to better adapt to this demographic change. Multicultural education is viewed as a method of adaptation. An effective way for the future recreation professional to gain initial exposure to the elements of diversity is through university and college curriculum. One major proposition discussed is that recreation educators need to include more multicultural education perspectives in the core recreation curriculum and not assume the topics will be adequately covered in the general education curriculum. This inclusion helps ensure that future recreation professionals receive profession-specific education regarding diverse ethnic/cultural groups and their impact on professional practice.

An assertive effort from educators toward a more inclusive recreation curriculum will benefit all and best prepare future recreation professionals for a society with increasingly diverse cultures. With the help of the educators and the students, it is hoped that we can learn together and create a better understanding of other cultures through recreation therapy.

Recreation professionals have a professional obligation to provide optimal services for their clients. To do so, recreation therapists must appropriately address cultural and ethnic variations that might impact the leisure experience. Leisure service educators should ensure that sufficient multicultural educational experiences are incorporated into the recreation curriculum and into the classes they teach. Recreation therapists can accomplish multicultural inclusion through several different approaches, including the contributions approach, the additive approach, the transformation approach, and the problem-solving social action approach.

Finally, attention was given to cultural considerations in client assessment. The recreation therapist should consider a critical evaluation of assessment instruments as they relate to culturally different people. In addition, self-appraisal — when a recreation therapist examines personal and professional issues — was mentioned as an important component in the overall assessment process. Also, the informal interaction between the recreation therapist and the culturally different client was presented as a means of developing and enhancing a closer therapist-client relationship. Finally, an interview guide was proposed to aid the recreation therapist in the assessment of culturally different individuals. Using these tools should provide therapists with the kind of information they need to provide effective, culturally aware treatment.

References

Adelman, C. 1992. *Tourist in Our Own Land.* Washington, DC: U.S. Department of Education.

Aguilar, T. 1990. Towards the Inclusion of Multicultural Issues in Leisure Studies Curricular. *Schole 5*: 41-52.

Aldag, T. & Sterns, R. 1991. *Management.* Cincinnati, OH: South-Western Publishing Co.

Altbach, P. & Lometey, K. 1991. *The Racial Crisis in American Higher Education.* Albany, NY: State University of NY Press.

Amaro, H., Beckman, L., & Mays, V. 1987. A Comparison of Black and White Women Entering Alcoholism Treatment. *Journal of Studies on Alcoholism 48*(3): 220-227.

American Council on Education. 1983. *A Nation at Risk: A Report of the Commission on Minority Participation in Education and American Life.* Washington, DC: American Council on Education.

American Council on Education. 1988. *One Third of a Nation: A Report of the Commission on Minority Participation in Education and American Life.* Washington, DC: American Council on Education.

American Therapeutic Recreation Association. 2000. *Standards for the Practice of Therapeutic Recreation and Self-assessment Guide.* ATRA Patient's/Client's Bill of Rights.

American Therapeutic Recreation Association. 2008. ATRA Board Approved Statements. Retrieved from www.atra-online.com/displaycommon.cfm?an=subarticlenbr=86 on September 24, 2010.

Andersen, M. 1988. Moving Our Minds: Studying Women of Color and Restructuring Sociology. *Teaching Sociology 16*(4): 123-132.

Aponte, F. A. & Crouch, T. R. 1995. The Changing Ethnic Profile of the United States. In *Psychological Interventions and Cultural Diversity*, edited by J. F. Aponte, R. Y. Rivers, & J. Wohl, 1-20. Boston, MA: Allyn Press.

Applebee, A., Langer, J., and Mullis, I. 1987. *The Nation's Report Card: Learning to be Literate in America: Reading.* Princeton, NJ: Education Testing Service.

Armstrong, K. L. 1998. Ten Strategies to Employ When Marketing to Black Consumers. *Sports Marketing Quarterly 7*(3): 11-18.

Arrendondo, P. 1985. Cross Cultural Counselor Education and Training. In
    Handbook for Cross Cultural Counseling and Therapy, edited by P.
    Pederson, 281-290. Westport, CT: Greenwood Press.

Asbury, C. A., Walker, S., Maholmes, V., Rackley, R., & White, S. 1991.
    *Disability Prevalence and Demographic Association among Race/Ethnic
    Minority Populations in the United States: Implications for the 21st
    Century*. Washington, DC: Howard University Research Training Center.

Associated Press. 2009. Surgeon General: More Minority Doctors Needed.
    Retrieved from www.usatoday.com/news/health/2009-12-03-minorities-
    doctors_N.htm. Referenced 24 Feb 2010.

Astin, A. W. 1977. *Four Critical Years*. San Francisco, CA: Jossey Bass,
    Publishing Co.

Atkins, B. J. 1999. An Asset-Oriented Approach to Cross-Cultural Issues:
    Blacks in Rehabilitation. *Journal of Applied Rehabilitation Counseling
    19*(4): 45-49.

Austin, D. R. 2004. *Therapeutic Recreation: Processes and Techniques* (5th
    ed.). Champaign, IL: Sagamore Publishing.

Banks, J. 1994. *An Introduction to Multicultural Education*. Needham Heights,
    MA: Allyn and Bacon.

Bernal, M. & Padilla, A. 1982. Status of Minority Curricula and Training in
    Clinical Psychology. *American Psychologist 37*: 780-787.

Bialeschki, D. 1992. The State of Parks, Recreation and Leisure Studies
    Curricula. *Parks and Recreation 27*(7): 72-76.

Blackwell, J. 1987. *Mainstreaming Outsiders: The Production of Black
    Professionals*. Bayside, NY: General Hall, Publishing Co.

Blake, M. & Gilbert, J. 2010. Black Computer Scientist in Academe: An
    Endangered Species? *The Chronicle of Higher Education Diversity*.
    September *24*: B35 – B37.

Bloom, A. 1987. *The Closing of the American Mind*. New York: Touchstone.

Bowe, F. 1992. *Adults with Disabilities: A Portrait*. Washington, DC:
    President's Committee on Employment of People with Disabilities.

Brown, S. V. 1988. *Increasing Minority Faculty: An Elusive Goal*. Princeton,
    NJ: Education Testing Service.

burlingame. j. & Blaschko, T. M. 2010. *Assessment Tools for Recreational
    Therapy and Related Fields* (Fourth Ed). Enumclaw, WA: Idyll Arbor.

Butt, K. L., & M. L. Pahonos. 1995. Why We Need a Multicultural Focus in our
    Schools. *Journal of Physical Education, Recreation and Dance 66*(1) 48-
    52.

Campinha-Bacote, J. 1998. *The Process of Cultural Competence in the Delivery of Healthcare Services: A Culturally Competent Model of Care* (3rd ed.) Cincinnati, OH: Transcultural C.A.R.E. Associates.

Carr, D. & Williams, D. 1993. Understanding the Role of Ethnicity in Outdoor Recreation Experiences. *Journal of Leisure Research 25*(1): 22-28.

Casas, J. 1982. Counseling Psychology in the Marketplace: The Status of Ethnic Minorities. *The Counseling Psychologist 37*: 780-787.

Chachkin, N. J. 1989. Testing in Elementary and Secondary Schools: Can Miscue Be Avoided? In *Test Policy and the Politics of Opportunity Allocation: The Workplace and the Law,* edited by B. Gifford, 163-187. Boston, MA: Kluwer Academic Publishers.

Cheek, N., Field, D., & Burdge, W. 1976. *Leisure and Recreation Places.* Ann Arbor, MI: Ann Arbor Science.

Chronicle of Higher Education. 2012. *Almanac of Higher Education 2012-13. Vol. XI, No 1., August 31, 2012*

Conrad, C., editor. 1985. *ASHE Reader on Academic Programs in Colleges and Universities.* Lexington, MA: Ginn Press.

Copeland, E. J. 1982. Minority Populations and Traditional Counseling Programs: Some Alternatives. *Counselor Education and Supervision 23*(3): 10-15.

D'Andrea, M., & Daniels, J. 1991. Exploring the Different Levels of Multicultural Counseling Training Programs in Counselor Education. *Journal of Counseling and Development 70*(1): 78-84.

Developmental Disabilities and Bill of Rights Act of 2002. Retrieved from http://www.acf.hhs.gov/programs/add/ddact/DDA.html on March 24, 2012.

Devine, H., Roberts, M., Okaya, A., & Xiong, Y. M. 2006. Our Lives Were Healthier Before: Focus Groups with African American, American Indian, Hispanic/Latino, Hmong People with Diabetes. *Health Promotion Practice 7*(1): 47–55.

Dieser, R. & Wilson, J. 2002. Learning to Listen: Crossing Ethnic Lines to Deliver Therapeutic Recreation Services. *Parks and Recreation* May 2002, 54–59

Doyle, E. 2008. Toward a Culturally Competent Health Education Workforce. In *Cultural Competence in Health Education and Health Promotion,* edited by M. Perez and R. Luquis, 163– 181. San Francisco, CA: Jossey-Bass.

D'Souza, D. 1995. *The End of Racism.* New York: The Free Press.

Dwyer, J. & Hutchinson, R. 1990. Outdoor Recreation Participation and Preferences by Black and White Chicago Households. In *Social Science and*

Natural Resource Management, edited by J. Vinning, 49-67. Boulder, CO: Westview Press.

Educational Testing Service. 1988. *A Summary of Data Collected from Graduate Record Examinations Test Takers During 1986-1987 [Data Summary Report #2]*. Newark, NJ: Author.

Ennis, S., Rios-Vargas, M., & Albert, N. 2011. *The Hispanic Population: 2010. 2010 Census Briefs*. United States Census Bureau.

Fain, G. & Shank, J. 1989. Individual Assessment through Leisure Profile Construction. In *The Best of the Therapeutic Recreation Journal: Assessment*, 90-97. National Therapeutic Recreation Society.

Feagin, J. & Feagin, C. 1978. *Discrimination American Style: Institutional Racism and Sexism.* Englewood Cliffs, NJ: Prentice-Hall, Inc.

Feldman, K. & Newcomb, T. 1969. *The Impact of College on Students*. San Francisco, CA: Jossey Bass Publishing Co.

Ferguson, D. 1989. Assessment Interviewing Techniques: A Useful Tool in Developing Individual Program Plans. In *The Best of the Therapeutic Recreation Journal: Assessment,* 116-122. National Therapeutic Recreation Society.

Fischer, K. 2012. Many Foreign Students Find Themselves Friendless in the United States. *The Chronicle of Higher Education 58*(39): A23.

Fisher-Fishkin, S. 1995. The Multiculturalism of Traditional Culture. *Chronicle of Higher Education 61*(26): 48.

Fleming, J. W. 1995. Balancing the Scales of Opportunity in Health Care: Ensuring Racial and Ethnic Diversity in the Health Professions. *Healthcare Trends and Transition 6*(4): 24-32.

Floyd, M. & Gramann, J. 1993. Effects of Acculturation and Structural Assimilation in Resource-based Recreation: The Case of Mexican Americans. *Journal of Leisure Research 25*: 6-21.

Floyd, M., Gramann, J., & Saenz, R. 1993. Ethnic Variations and the Use of Public Outdoor Recreation Areas: The Case of Mexican Americans. *Leisure Sciences 15*: 83-98.

Floyd, M., McGuire, F., Shinew. K., & Noe, F. 1994. Race, Class and Leisure Activity Preferences: Marginality and Ethnicity Revisited. *Leisure Sciences 26*:158-173.

Gaff, J. 1983. Emerging Curricular Patterns. *Academic Programs in Colleges and Universities,* edited by C. Conrad. Lexington, MA: Ginn Press.

Garcia G. & Pearson, P. 1994. Assessment and Diversity. In *Review of Research in Education*, edited by L. D. Hammond, 344-391. Washington, DC: American Educational Research Association.

Getz, D. 2002. Increasing Cultural Competence in Therapeutic Recreation. In *Conceptual Foundations for Therapeutic Recreation,* edited by D. Austin, J. Datillo, and B. McCormick. State College, PA: Venture Publishing, Inc.

Goldman, R. E., Monroe, A. D., & Dube, C. E. 1996. Cultural Self-Awareness: A Component of Culturally Responsive Patient Care. *Annuals of Behavioral Science and Medical Education* 3: 37-46.

Gomez-Quinonez, J. 1977. *On Culture.* UCLA Chicano Studies Center Publications, Popular Series No. 1. Los Angeles, CA.

Gunn, S. L. and Peterson, C. A. 1978. *Therapeutic Recreation: Principles and Procedures*. Englewood Cliffs, NJ: Prentice Hall.

Hauser, P. 1962. *Demographic and ecological changes as factors in outdoor recreation: Trends in American living and outdoor recreation. [Outdoor Recreation Resources Review Commission, Study Report 22].* Washington, DC: U.S. Government Printing Office.

Hammond. 2010. *Hammond World Atlas (6th Ed).* Italy: Hammond World Atlas Corporation.

Healy, P. 1995. Bias in the Curriculum. *Chronicle of Higher Education 25*: 23-24.

Henderson, K., Bedini, L., & Bialeschki, D. 1993. Feminism and the Client-Therapist Relationship: Implications for Therapeutic Recreation. *Therapeutic Recreation Journal 27*(1): 33-43.

Hibbler, D. K., editor. 2002. *Unsilencing the Dialog: Voices of Minority Faculty*. Florida International University: Center for Urban Education and Innovation.

Hixson, L., Helper, B., & Kim, M. 2011. *The White Population: 2010. 2010 Census Briefs*. United States Census Bureau.

Hodgkinson, H. 1988. Proceedings from the National Conference of Civic Education '88: *The Context of 21st Century Civics and Citizenship.* Washington, DC, October 1988.

Hoeffel, E., Rastogi, S., Kim, M., & Shahid, H. 2012. *The Asian Population: 2010. 2010 Census Briefs.* United States Census Bureau.

Hogan-Hill, C., Gary-Williams, G., & Jackson, S. 1995. Diversity and Access: The Future of Allied Health Professions. *Healthcare Trends & Transition* 6(3):15-20.

Holland, J. 1992. The Effects of Faculty Involvement on African American
    Doctoral Students Choosing Careers in Higher Education. Unpublished
    doctoral dissertation. University of Wisconsin-Madison, WI.

Holland. J. 2002. *Black Recreation: A Historical Perspective.* Chicago, IL:
    Burnham, Inc.

Howe, C. 1989. Leisure Assessment Instrumentation in Therapeutic Recreation.
    In *The Best of the Therapeutic Recreation Journal Assessment.* National
    Therapeutic Recreation Society.

Humes, K., Jones, N., & Ramirez, R. 2011. *Overview of Race and Hispanic
    Origin: 2010.* Retrieved March 28, 2011, from
    http://www.census.gov/prod/cem2010/briefs/c2010br-02.pdf.

Hutchison, R. 1987. Ethnicity and Urban Recreation: Whites, Blacks, Hispanics
    in Chicago's Public Parks. *Journal of Leisure Research 19*: 205-222.

Hutchison, R. 1988. A Critique of Race, Ethnicity, and Social Class in Recent
    Leisure-Recreation Research. *Journal of Leisure Research 20*: 10-30.

Hutchison, R. & Fidel, K. 1984. Mexican-American Recreation Activities: A
    Reply to McMillen. *Journal of Leisure Research 16*: 344-349.

Indianapolis A. P. 2010. Nursing Home Ruling Halts Race-based Caregiver
    Choices. *The La Crosse Tribune*, August 24.

Jennings, J. 2011. Why is running so white? *Runner's World*, 92-99, 124-125.
    December.

Jordan, D. 1999. *Leadership in Leisure Services: Making a Difference.* State
    College, PA: Venture Publishing.

Katz, J. 1999. White Culture and Racism: Working for Organizational Change
    in the United States. *The Whiteness Papers No. 3, 5.* Roselle, NJ: Center for
    the Study of White American Culture.

Katz, J. & Hartnett, R. 1976. *Scholars in the Making: The Development of
    Graduate and Professional Students.* Cambridge, MA: Ballinger Publishing
    Co.

Kornegay, F. & Warren, D. 1969. *A Comparative Study of Life Styles and Social
    Attitudes of Middle Income Status Whites and Negroes in Detroit.* Detroit,
    MI: Detroit Urban League.

Kraus, R. & Shank, J. 1992. *Therapeutic Recreation Service: Principles and
    Practice (4th ed.).* Dubuque, IA: Wm. C. Brown Publishers.

La Crosse Tribune. 2012. More write in "other" on census forms. February, 1,
    2012

Lattanzi, J. & Purnell, L., editors. 2006. *Developing Cultural Competence in
    Physical Therapy Practice.* Philadelphia, PA: F. A. Davis Company.

Leininger, M. 1978. *Transcultural Nursing: Concepts, Theories, Research and Practices (2nd ed.)*. New York: MacGraw Hill, Inc.

Lenburg, C., Lipson, J., Demi, A., Blaney, D., Stern, P., Schulta, P., & Gage, L. 1995. *Promoting Cultural Competence in and through Nursing Education: A Critical Review and Comprehensive Plan for Action*. Washington, DC: American Academy of Nursing.

Lynch, E. & Hanson, M. 1997. Steps in the Right Direction: Implications for Interventionists. In *Developing Cross-Cultural Competence: A Guide for Working with Children and Their Families*, edited by E. Lynch and M. Hanson, 491-512. Baltimore, MD: Paul Brookes Publishing.

Mandela, N. 1995. *Long Walk to Freedom: The Autobiography of Nelson Mandela*. Boston, MA: Little, Brown and Company.

McCabe Smith, L. & Malkin, M. 1999. Multicultural issues for recreational therapist and other rehabilitation professionals. *Selected Papers from the 1999 Midwest Symposium on Therapeutic Recreation*, edited by G. Hitzhusen and L. Thomas, 99-103. Expanding Horizons in Therapeutic Recreation.

McDonald, J. & Hutchinson, I. 1987. Minority and Ethnic Variations in Outdoor Recreation Participation: Trends and Issues. *Therapeutic Recreation Journal 21*: 26-35.

McNeil, J, editor. 2002. *Be Safe: A Cultural Competency Model for African Americans*. Washington, DC: National Minority AIDS Education and Training Center.

Mercer, J. 1989. Alternative Paradigms for Assessment in a Pluralistic Society. In *Multicultural Education: Issues and Perspectives,* edited by J. A. Banks & C. A. M. Banks, 289-304. Boston, MA: Allyn & Bacon.

Mingle, J. R. 1987. *Focusing on Minorities: Trends in Higher Education Participation and Success*. Denver, CO: Education Commission of the States and the State Higher Education Executive Officers.

Molnar, A. 1987. *Social Issues and Education: Challenge and Responsibility*. Alexandria, VA: Association for Supervision and Curriculum Development.

Moore, M. & Moos, M. K. 2003. *Cultural Competence in the Care of Childbearing Families*. White Plains, NY: March of Dimes Birth Defects Foundation Education Services.

Mueller, E. & Gurin, G. 1962. *Participation in Outdoor Recreation: Factors Affecting the Demand Among American Adults*. Outdoor Recreation Resources Review Commission, Study Report 20. Washington, DC: U.S. Government Printing Office.

National Center for Education Statistics. 1988. *Education Indicators.* Washington, DC: U.S. Department of Education, Office of Educational Research and Improvement.

National Council for Therapeutic Recreation Certification. 2007. 2007 JOB analysis report. Retrieved from http:www.nctrc/documents/NCTRJAReport07.pdf on January 10, 2012.

National Council on Disability. 1993. *Meeting the Unique Needs of Minorities with Disabilities.* Available from http:www.ncd.gov/publications/1993/April261993.

National Council on Disability. 1999. *Lift Every Voice: Modernizing Disability Politics and Programs to Serve a Diverse Nation.* Available from http:www.ncd.gov/publications/1999/Dec11999.

National Outdoor Leadership School. 2012. NOLS to Lead African American Expedition on Denali. Available at http:www.nols.edu/news/. Accessed August 13, 2013.

Nuelinger, J. 1990. What Am I Doing? In *Assessment Tools for Recreation Therapy*, j. burlingame and T. Blaschko, 79-90. Enumclaw, WA: Idyll Arbor, Inc.

National Council for Therapeutic Recreation Certification. 2007. *2007 Job Analysis Report.* Retrieved from http:www.nctrc.org/documents/NCTRCJAReport07.pdf.

National Council on Disability. 1999. *National Council on Disability: Living, Learning, and Earning.* Retrieved from http:www.ncd.gov/newsroom/publications/1999/Dec.11999

O'Leary, J. & Benjamin, P. 1981. *Ethnic Variations in Leisure Behaviors, Studies, Theories and Directions for Future Research.* Chicago University & Purdue University: Cooperative Research Project U.S. Forest Experimental Station,

Outdoor Recreation Resources Review Commission. 1962. Participation in Outdoor Recreation: Factors Affecting Demand among American Adults in Recreation. *(Report to the President and the Congress. Vol. 20).* Washington, DC: U.S. Government Printing Office.

Padilla, A. 1979. Critical Factors in the Testing of Hispanics: A Review and Some Suggestions for the Future. In *National Institute of Education, Testing, Teaching, and Learning: Report of a Conference on Research in Testing*, 219-244. Washington, DC: U.S. Government Printing Office.

Pallas, A., Natriello, G., & McDill, E. 1989. The Changing Nature of the Disadvantaged Population: Current Dimensions and Future Trends. *Education Researcher 18*(5): 16-22

Pantages, T. & Creedon, C. 1978. Studies of College Attrition: 1950-1975. *Review of Educational Research 48*: 49-101.

Parker, M. Woodrow. 1998. *Consciousness-Raising: A Primer for Multicultural Counseling*. Springfield, IL: Charles C. Thomas Publishing.

Peregoy, J. & Diesler, R. 1995. *Multicultural Aspects of Therapeutic Recreation.* Unpublished raw data.

Peregoy, J. & Diesler, R. 1997. Multicultural Awareness in Therapeutic Recreation: Hamlet Living. *Therapeutic Recreation Journal 31*: 173-187.

Peregoy, J., Schliebner, C., & Diesler, R. 1997. Diversity Issues in Therapeutic Recreation. In *Issues in Therapeutic Recreation: Towards the New Millennium,* edited by D. Compton, 275-298. Champaign, IL: Sagamore Publishing.

Perez, M. 2008. Strategies, Practices, and Models for Delivering Culturally Competent Health Education Programs. In *Cultural Competence in Health Education and Health Promotion*, edited by M. Perez & R. Luquis, 183-200. San Francisco, CA: Jossey-Bass.

Peterson, C. & Gunn, S. 1984. *Therapeutic Recreation Program Design: Principles and Procedures* (2nd ed.). Englewood Cliffs, NJ: Prentice-Hall, Inc.

Philipp, S. 1993. Racial Differences in the Perceived Attractiveness of Tourism Destinations, Interest, and Cultural Resources. *Journal of Leisure Research 25*(3): 290-304.

Pinderhughes, E. 1989. *Understanding, Race, Ethnicity, and Power: The Key to Efficacy in Clinical Practice.* New York: Free Press.

Ponterotto, J. & Casas, J. 1987. In Search of Multicultural Competencies Within Counselor Education. *Journal of Counseling and Development 64*: 430-434.

Purnell, L. & Paulanka, B. 1998. *Transcultural Health Care: A Culturally Competent Approach.* Philadelphia, PA: F. A. Davis, Co.

Rastogi, S., Johnson, T., Hoeffel, E., & Drewery, M. 2011. *The Black Population: 2010. 2010 Census Briefs.* United States Census Bureau.

Shils, E. 1982. *The Academic Ethic.* Chicago, IL: University of Chicago Press.

Schlesinger, A. 1992. *The Disuniting of America: Reflections of a Multicultural Society.* New York: W.W. Norton & Co.

Smith, E. 1982. Counseling Psychology in the Marketplace: The Status of Ethnic Minorities. *The Counseling Psychologist 10*: 61-67.

Stumbo, N. 1991. Selected Assessment Resources: A Review of Instruments and References. In *Annual in Therapeutic Recreation,* edited by M. Crawford & J. Card, 8-24. Reston: American Alliance for Health, Physical Education, Recreation and Dance.

Stumbo, N. 2001. Revisited: Issues and Concerns in Therapeutic Recreation Assessment. In *Professional Issues in Therapeutic Recreation: On Competence and Outcomes,* edited by N. Stumbo, 215-235. Champaign, IL: Sagamore.

Sylvester, C., Voelkl, J., & Ellis, G. 2001. *Therapeutic Recreation Programming: Theory and Practice.* State College, PA: Venture Publishing.

Sue, D. W. 1981. *Counseling the Culturally Different: Theory and Practice.* New York: John Wiley and Sons.

Sue, D., & Sue, D. 1990. *Counseling the Culturally Different: Theory and Practice* (2nd Ed). New York: John Wiley and Sons.

The Joint Commission. 2010. *The Joint Commission: Advancing Effective Communication, Cultural Competence, and Patient- and Family-Centered Care: A Roadmap for Hospitals.* Oakland Terrace, IL: The Joint Commission.

Trokie, R. 1984. SCALP: Social and Cultural Aspects of Language Proficiency. In *Language Proficiency and Academic Achievement,* edited by C. Rivera, 44-54. Avon, England: Multicultural Matters.

Trower, C. & Chait, R. 2002. Faculty Diversity. Harvard Magazine. March/April.

Turner, C. & Meyers, S. 2000. *Faculty of Color in Academe: Bittersweet Success.* Boston: Allyn and Bacon.

U.S. Census Bureau. 2004. *U.S. Interim Projections by Age, Sex, Race, and Hispanic Origin.* Retrieved from www.censusus.gov/ipc/www/usinterimproj/.

U.S. Census Bureau News. 2004. U.S. Dept of Commerce, Washington, D.C., Newsroom release March 1, 2004.

U.S. Department of Health and Human Services Office of Minority Health (2007). *National Standards on culturally and linguistically appropriate services (CLAS).* Retrieved from http:minorityhealth.hhs.gov/templates/browse.aspx?lvl=2&lvID=15

Vawter, D. E., Culhane-Pera, K. A., Babbitt, B., Xiong, P., & Solberg, M. 2003. A Model For Culturally Responsive Health Care. In *Healing by Heart: Clinical and Ethical Case Stories of Hmong Families and Western Providers,* edited by K. A. Culhane-Pera, D. E. Vawter, P. Xiong, B.

Babbitt, & M. M. Solberg, 297-356. Nashville, TN: Vanderbilt University Press.

Ward, K. 1994. Moving Beyond Adding Race, Class, and Gender and Stirring. *Schole 9*: 55-61.

Walker, S. 1998. *Building Bridges to Independence*. Report prepared for the President's Committee on Employment of People with Disabilities. Washington, DC: U.S. Government Printing Office.

Washburne, R. 1978. Black Under-Participation in Wild Land Recreation: Alternative Explanations. *Leisure Sciences 1*: 175-189.

Washington Associated Press. 2012. Many write in "other" on census forms. *La Crosse Tribune*, February 2.

Wendling, R. 1981. Black/White Differences in Outdoor Recreation Behavior: State-of-the-art and Recommendations for Management and Research, 106-117. Proceedings of the Conference on Social Research in National Parks and Wildlife Areas '81. March 21-22, 1980, Great Smokey Mountains National Park, Gatlinburg, TN.

West, C. 1993. *Race Matters*. New York: Random House, Inc.

Wilson, K. P. 2002. *Campfires of Freedom: The Camp Life of Black Soldiers during the Civil War*. Burton, OH: The Kent State University Press.

Part II. Cultural Descriptions

The second part of the book will address demographic data, significant historical information, general cultural group information, and cultural and recreational observances of the following racial/ethnic groups: African Americans, Chinese Americans, Japanese Americans, Hmong Americans, Mexican Americans, and Puerto Rican Americans. Many factors impact the recreation participation of individuals affiliated with these groups.

It is important to note that not all members of a particular racial or ethnic group may identify with all of the group's cultural customs. This identification will vary depending on numerous factors, including acculturation, assimilation, community life, parenting, education, access to services, past experiences in healthcare, amount of trust in the healthcare system, communication barriers, role models, mentoring, age, and so forth. Treatment implications for recreation therapists are highlighted in italics.

6. African Americans

African Americans are United States citizens who trace their ancestry to the black populations of Africa. Most are the direct descendants of captured blacks who endured slavery in the United States. The 2012 census reported that African Americans comprise the second largest ethnic minority group (behind Latinos) in the U.S., at over 13% of the U.S. population (Rastogl et al. 2011). The 2010 census indicates more than 38 million African Americans reside in the United States. Thirty-eight million may not appear significant in comparison to the total U.S. population, which is more than 318 million. However, when compared to the total number of citizens in smaller countries, 38 million people is not insignificant. For example, in comparison, American blacks outnumber the total number of citizens in Ghana (20 million), Belgium (10 million), Switzerland (7 million), Iraq (24 million), Senegal (10 million), Kenya (32 million), and Israel (6 million) (Collins 2005).

Some Important Historical Dates for African Americans

Most African Americans' ancestors came from Africa prior to arriving in America. In 1619, twenty Africans arrived in Jamestown, Virginia, and were forcibly settled as involuntary workers (Ashante & Mattson 1991). Subsequently, many more Africans were captured and brought to America as slaves. "The period of slavery in the United States was a magnificent yet horrendous era" (Holland 2002, 54). It was magnificent because America was in the early stages of development and growing significantly as a nation. It was horrendous because of what slaves had to endure in helping the nation prosper. Numerous accounts tell of the inhumane mistreatment of slaves during the antebellum period. The impact of slavery on blacks was painful and degrading, and most were forced to abandon much of their African culture, including their play, recreation, and leisure, as they adapted to slave life in America (Holland 2002). So powerful was the conduct during slavery that the impact of such treatment continues to be painful for some contemporary African Americans who continue to harbor resentment for America's actions during the slavery period. Such treatment is difficult to erase from the passing down of cultural information from generation to generation.

In 1861, the South seceded from the Union and the Civil War began. In 1863, President Lincoln issued the Emancipation Proclamation. In 1865, the Thirteenth Amendment to the U.S. Constitution outlawed slavery in the U.S. This amendment provided that "Neither slavery nor involuntary servitude, except as a punishment for crime whereof the party shall have been duly convicted, shall exist within the United States, or any place subject to their jurisdiction" (Thirteenth Amendment to the U.S. Constitution 2012).

Although free from bondage, life in America for the freemen continued to be filled with mistreatment, prejudice, and discrimination. Many were forced to remain close to one another for safety and protection from some whites. The vast majority were very poor and severely undereducated. Even with their freedom, most of the newly freed backs remained mostly segregated from whites. The law of the land was separation between blacks and whites, officially recognized in 1869 with the Supreme Court's *Plessy vs. Ferguson* decision, which affirmed a separate-but-equal doctrine. Although the separation continued, the policy did not provide equality for blacks. In 1954, with the *Brown vs. Board of Education* decision, the Supreme Court overruled *Plessy,* declaring racial segregation in schools unconstitutional.

In 1963, Dr. Martin Luther King Jr. gave his famous "I have a dream" speech, advocating equality between the races. In 1964 President Lyndon B. Johnson signed the Civil Rights Act of 1964, its intent being the guarantee of equality among the races. Nevertheless, due in part to the legacy of slavery, racism, and discrimination, as a group African Americans remained at a disadvantage — economically, educationally, and socially — relative to whites in America.

Traditionally in the United States, with the exception of California and Texas, the majority of African Americans have lived east of the Mississippi River (Asante & Mattson 1991). The 2010 census indicated that 55.6% of African Americans lived in the South, 17.8 % lived in the Northeast, 17.9% lived in the Midwest, while 8.8% resided in the Western states (however, California has the fifth-largest African American population, behind only New York, Texas, Georgia, and Florida) (Rastogl et al. 2011).

African American Culture and Customs

The African American population is a diverse group — many are descendants of slaves who came from different countries of Africa's west coast in the mid-seventeenth century. Blacks from different West African tribes, including the Ashante, Ebo, and Yorobo tribes, were forced into slavery. Though all were from Africa, they were very different people from different regions, different tribes, and with different customs (Asante & Mattson 1991). The institution of slavery forced them to abandon many of their old ways, stripping them of many of their African customs.

As a diverse group with different personal and group experiences, there have been several preferred names for this group in America, including *African American*, *black*, *person of color*, *negro*, and *colored*. The terms *colored* and *negro* might be preferred by some older people, while *African American*, *black*, and *person of color* are more often preferred by the current majority.

The recreation therapist may need to ask the patient/client for the preferred group affiliation name or term that the individual identifies with.

Unlike some racial groups, within the African American population are varying degrees of skin color, from light brown to darker brown and even a few individuals with very light skin, who identify with black culture. Dark-skinned people from the Caribbean may also identify with African American culture, but most of them prefer to be recognized by more specific terms (Haitian, Jamaican, Dominican, and so on). Newer immigrants with dark skin from Africa (such as Nigerian and Tanzanian individuals) generally have little in common with African American culture, although they face many of the issues African Americans do.

Contemporary life for many African Americans continues to be deeply rooted in customs and traditions influenced by the history of slavery and the experiences that slaves endured in the U.S. after slavery. A relatively recent remnant of this legacy may be exemplified in a comment by Harry Reid, a U.S. senator from Nevada. During the 2008 presidential campaign, Senator Reid made comments to the authors of *Game Change* (a book about American politics) that Barack Obama — who was running for President of United States at the time — was "a light skinned African American with no negro dialect." (Heileman & Halperin 2010). Reid was commenting on qualities that he felt would help an African American become the first black president in the United States: a light-skinned complexion and speaking proper English. Such biased ideals based on skin color were evident even during the slavery period; it was common knowledge that lighter-skinned slaves often received better treatment and could be given less physically demanding tasks by slave owners than their darker-skinned brethren received (Holland 2002).

Even though African Americans have made significant and monumental strides in contemporary America, there are successes that African Americans have yet to achieve. Many African Americans can still recall the first time an African American accomplished certain milestones in America. Indeed, African Americans continue to encounter a number of "firsts" since the end of slavery in 1865. Examples include Jackie Robinson, the first black allowed to play in major league baseball

(1947); Thurgood Marshall, the first black Supreme Court justice (1967); Arthur Ashe, the first black man inducted into the International Tennis Hall of Fame (1985); Condoleezza Rice, the first African American woman secretary of state (2005); and Barack Obama, the first African American president of the United States of America (2008).

Nevertheless, due to a history of discrimination and despite some successes in sports and entertainment, negative stereotypes have been applied to African Americans, including that they are less intelligent, oversexed, less motivated, lazy, overly angry, aggressive, and hostile, and that they have poor hygiene, prefer government assistance, have superior athletic prowess, and have naturally superior dancing and singing ability (Duke 1991; Wiener 1991; Parker 1991; Manning 1991). Many African Americans face these stereotypes, which continue in America. When a person has to defend against such stereotypes, it may produce an emotional drain (D'Souza 1995).

African Americans are represented in all socioeconomic groups in America. Regardless, as a group, a number of negative issues and stereotypes continue to impact some contemporary African Americans, including discrimination in employment and housing (Bell 2004; Rowan 1993) and healthcare treatment. Very troubling is the concept of racial profiling, which is thought of in several ways, but is most often thought to occur when law enforcement inappropriately considers a person's race in deciding with whom and how to intervene. For example, some African Americans, especially young black males, have complained of being pulled over more often when driving certain types of vehicles and when driving through particular areas and neighborhoods (some African Americans have coined this "driving while black.") In addition, there continues to be evidence that blacks tend to be watched more intently when they are engaged in certain activities, like shopping (Elder 2000).

It may be important for the recreation therapists to determine if, or to what extent, the patient/client feels that such stereotypes and behavior have affected them in their recreation participation. The ethnicity theory discussed in Part I may shed light on "expected" activity participation and interest. For example, some activities have traditionally been considered "white activities," such as swimming, golf, hockey, ice skating, and skiing. As such, the therapist might expect African Americans not to have interest these pursuits.

It's important to note that African Americans are a highly diverse group in terms of socioeconomic status, geographic location, and physical appearance. Yet they are a culturally distinct group bound by similar ideological unity, values, and beliefs (much influenced by treatment before and after slavery). In light of their history, as a cultural group African Americans have a strong sense of collective group orientation (McNeil 2002), probably due to survival mechanisms developed during slavery. During slavery, it was imperative for slaves to work together. By working closely together, deep and enduring cultural relationships were formed that had lasting bonds for those of African ancestry. These cultural bonds continue today.

African American cultural ethnology and views of the world were and are woven together, and they help provide meaning and order not only to African Americans' historical experiences, but to their contemporary experiences as well. An appreciation of these cultural elements is a prerequisite to understanding and interpreting black patterns of behavior (Butler 1992). It may be difficult for some to understand, but among some African Americans, no words may be necessary when communicating with others — whether friends or not — of the same race. One look and they can discern what the other is trying to convey.

If recreation therapists are to work effectively with African Americans in treatment, they must use models that recognize and acknowledge the African American view of the world, their behavioral and lifestyle patterns, and their coping and problem-solving methods.

Music and dance are often considered important aspects in African American culture. African American music is one of the most enduring African American cultural influences in the U.S. today. Many different musical genres have been developed and are enjoyed by blacks (and others), including gospel, jazz, blues, R & B, and rap. However, African Americans' taste in music can be varied; many enjoy all types of music, including classical, country, alternative, rock, or folk. Like music, dance has been significant in black culture. Many dances originated in African American communities, including the Twist, the Mashed Potato, Funky Chicken, the Bump, Tootsie Roll, break dancing, and krumpin'.

Similar to the diversity in music and dance, there is great diversity in African Americans with regards to personal presentation and style. Preparing people to stand on their own and be independent is valued. The importance of independence is passed on to African American children. Children are valued because they are the future of the race. Children are reared to be obedient and respectful to older people. Traditionally, children are often taught to address adults formally, beginning with titles like Mr., Mrs., Ms., Miss., Aunt, Uncle, or Reverend as an indicator of respect for their position in the community and as adults (Wright 2001). Furthermore, African American children are taught a sense of ethnic pride and positive esteem (Wright 2001). This pride might be manifested in communication (speaking), behavior (assertiveness), and clothing style (dress). Many young people, especially young men, walk with a particular pace and stride that is distinctive. In some communities this distinctive walk has been referred to as "strutting" or "strolling."

Likewise, there is much diversity in hairstyles and looks worn by African Americans, including the afro, braids, cornrows, baldness, dreadlocks, fades, bantu/zulu knots, waves, the jheri curl, and natural. A stereotype that sometimes prevails is the supposed correlation between a particular style or appearance and aggression or behavior. One recent example of this stereotype: the 2012 nationally publicized case of the killing of Trayvon Martin in Sanford, Florida. Seventeen-year-old Trayvon, on his way home after buying candy at a local store, was shot and killed by a volunteer neighborhood watchman, George Zimmerman, because Zimmerman believed Trayvon looked suspicious. One of Zimmerman's reasons for being suspicious was that Trayvon was wearing a hoodie. (Hoodies are sweatshirts with hoods — the hoods are often pulled up over the head. Many urban gang members and some undesirables have been known to wear hoodies.) An altercation between Martin and Zimmerman occurred, resulting in the shooting death of Martin. By all accounts, Martin was not a gang member. He was a typical African American teenager walking home from a food store. Martin was later found to have been unarmed. Zimmerman was tried and acquitted based on his claim that he acted in self-defense. The verdict led to protests across the country that blacks are not treated fairly in U.S. courts.

Recreation therapists should note that there is no empirical evidence that indicates a relationship between music preferences, dance ability, presentation style, or hair appearance with some stereotypical beliefs or perceived behaviors of African Americans.

Many African American patients/clients are sensitive to hasty assessment and treatment by non-African Americans (McNeil 2002). This relates to the generally broad communal nature of African American culture. As such, many African Americans may feel that non-African Americans really do not know much about them, and feel significant time is needed to understand their particular issues.

It is important for the recreation therapist to consider the amount of time given to dialogue or interactions to better bridge the therapist-patient/client gap. For example, in gathering assessment data, giving someone a piece of paper and having them fill out a questionnaire may not be as effective as investing more time in a dialogue.

Communication between recreation therapists and African Americans should be an area of focus. When some African Americans communicate with healthcare professionals, eye contact, touch, facial expression, and language become relevant (McNeil 2002). Communication styles and preferences are varied within the African American community. Some African American communication styles may be considered assertive. For some blacks, especially those living in urban-deprived neighborhoods, verbal ability (the ability to assert oneself confidently) contributes as much as physical strength in gaining prestige. In other words, in some African American communities, some may feel it is important to portray a presence of high confidence in order to be respected. For many, nonverbal communication (expressions and gesturing) is expressive and animated. Direct eye contact without staring is acceptable for many African Americans; however, more sustained eye contact may be viewed as being aggressive. In addition, some older African Americans may not maintain eye contact with people in higher authority positions.

Recreation therapists should be aware that certain cultural norms may also impact their communication with some African Americans. Recreation therapists need to analyze and understand the preferred communication preferences of each client/patient in order to discover the most appropriate strategy for effective two-way communication.

African Americans may speak standard English and black English (which has also been referred to as Ebonics). Further, it is not uncommon for some blacks, even those who are highly educated and successful, to use both styles, depending on the particular social environment. The use of Ebonics has created controversy in the academic community and in black communities, as some mainstream educators and black community leaders have refused to acknowledge it as a legitimate form of communication. Regardless of its acceptance, many blacks continue to use Ebonics or non-standardized English when communicating. For instance, phrases such as "Mama an em were sayin' it's hot," "That hurted me," or "Cause you always gon be da man" are used often and are very common in African American communities. Also, some words may be pronounced differently. Commonly, some African Americans pronounce "the" as "de," or rather than saying "these," some may say "dese." Further, some words or phrases might be used in ways that have different meanings than standard English. For example "fat" in standard English most often means "overweight," whereas "phat" (pronounced the same) could be used by African Americans to indicate attractiveness or beauty, in addition to meaning "overweight." Following is a list of words or phrases in standard English and their counterparts or meanings that *may be* used by some — primarily young — African Americans.

Standard English	Other (African American) meaning
Tight	Things are fine
Grill	A person's face
Bad	Good
Bad boys	Things or objects
Cheesin'	Smiling
Playa	An up-to-date person, friend
Benjamins	Money
"You sick!"	You are wild or unpredictable
Hooptie or Whip	Automobile
Boo	Girlfriend or significant partner
Do you	Take action
Bounce	Get going

Recreation therapists should be aware that some words may have different meanings, depending upon the words' cultural contexts. Simultaneously, the therapist may need to listen more carefully to the client until the possible communication gaps are narrowed, anticipating the possibility of a somewhat longer encounter. Further, the recreation therapist may need to ask the individual — possibly more often than is typical — to repeat and clarify terms that the therapist is unfamiliar with. Therapist should note that cross-racial dialogue and communication can be a difficult skill to master. The most efficient ways to enhance skills in these areas are through practice and thoughtful consideration.

In the communication process, some African Americans may speak loudly, especially when anxious, excited, or trying to get a point across (McNeil 2002). Speaking loudly to others is often interpreted as being angry or aggressive.

Although this interpretation is often correct with most individuals, recreation therapists should not always interpret the loudness as anger or aggression, when in fact speaking loudly, especially in the company of friends, does not always indicate anger or aggressiveness. For some African Americans, depending on the situation, these actions are simply established routines they have learned as methods of communication.

In many African American families, communication is open and characterized by trust. However, for people outside the family or close friends, communication is often limited and family matters are viewed as private, not to be discussed beyond a limited number of people.

If the recreation therapist can gain the trust of the patient/client, they are more likely to develop a more truthful communication.

Another important cultural dimension is the African American church. The church has always had an important place in African American culture. Especially during slavery, the church was where blacks were — and felt — most free. During slavery, church service usually occurred on Sunday. Sundays were cherished by those in bondage, because slaves could be free from mandatory labor on Sundays.

The church was a place where slaves could express themselves more freely through congregation, testifying, preaching, prayers, and songs. Contemporary African Americans are members of many different faiths, including Baptist, Catholic, Protestant, Lutheran, Seventh Day Adventist, Muslim, and others. The church continues to hold a privileged place for many African Americans today. For many African Americans, their inner strength comes from trusting in God, and the church has played an integral part in African Americans' development and survival. In many black churches, they say that whatever happens is "God's will."

It is important for the recreation therapist to acknowledge the patient's/client's spiritual worldview. Some may view future occurrences as out of their control, regardless of the amount of effort that is put into attempting to control an outcome. No matter what types of interventions are used or recommended by the recreation therapist, some African Americans may feel the future is not in their control.

The Hip Hop Movement

The hip hop movement has had a definitive impact on many African American youth, other youths, and even some adults in their likes, dislikes, play, recreation, and leisure. The impetus of hip hop includes music, storytelling, and the use of rap music to address some of life's issues, such as style, racism, oppression, poverty, and so on. Many may believe that hip hop encompasses only music, particularly rap music. However, hip hop is more than rap music. Hip hop includes not only music but also dance, language, literature, communication, dress, social interactions, and sexuality. Some adults have a negative attitude regarding hip hop and think of it as a negative fad that will quickly fade away. The perceived negative side of hip hop is sometimes portrayed in the music genre by musical groups singing and rapping about illegal drugs, guns, pimping, prostitution, violence, and gangs. Hip hop music often glorifies these actions, as they have a definite impact on many youth and adults. As a consequence, many professionals may refuse to acknowledge the cultural legitimacy of hip hop culture.

However, hip hop has made its mark, and many prominent businesses have jumped onto the hip hop bandwagon, cashing in on the culture, noticing its influence not only on urban black youth but also on youth and adults of all races and ethnicities around the world. One example of the impact of hip hop is in literature. Many book publishers publish hip hop (also referred to as "urban") novels. These novels, although fiction, tell stories of life situations primarily set in urban areas. Inundated with urban slang, these novels tend to describe life circumstances that many black youth relate to better than they do more mainstream books. Many black youth read these exciting novels filled with graphic text and rather unpredictable story lines. They're not truly academic books, but have an impact on African American readers because they relate better to the storylines. The reality is that hip hop can mold attitudes while impacting the cultural realities of the mostly young hip hop generation.

Because hip hop has this ability, professionals would be wise to not only acknowledge hip hop but also find ways to address its impact on professional relationships. Some of the young men and women that recreation therapists interact with will bring a background that reflects elements of hip hop, and neither the recreation therapists' personal backgrounds nor their ages are an excuse for the therapists to be ignorant of this phenomenon.

One practical way to look at hip hop is to view it as professionals have tended to view other critical life skills. For example, if noteworthy and current issues in society are obesity, time management, or sexual behavior, then individuals will tend to read books, attend conferences, or look to people with knowledge or expertise to help them better understand those issues. Recreation therapists need not necessarily either accept or reject hip hop. Nevertheless, recreation therapists should seek an understanding of this genre as a means of better understanding people whose lives may be in some ways governed and affected by the movement.

Holidays, Celebrations, and Recreation

African Americans celebrate and acknowledge traditional U.S. holidays, including New Year's Eve and Day, Valentine's Day, Presidents' Day, Easter, Memorial Day, Mother's Day, Father's Day, Fourth of July, Labor Day, Halloween, Thanksgiving, and Christmas. In addition, a few other holiday and celebration periods have gained prominence with some African Americans and other Americans. These will be discussed below.

Black History Month

In the U.S., Black History Month is celebrated annually in February. In theory, Black History Month celebrates important people and events in the history of African Americans. The remembrance originated in 1926 by historian Carter G. Woodson as Negro History Week. Woodson selected the second week of February because it marked the birthdays of two Americans who greatly influenced the lives and social situation of African Americans: former President Abraham Lincoln and Frederick Douglas, a former slave and abolitionist. Today, Black History Month is celebrated via school events, community events, television shows, concerts, special programs, speakers, plays, and dinners. (Black History Month 2012).

Juneteenth Day

Juneteenth Day is celebrated in June. For many enslaved blacks and their heirs, Juneteenth Day is the equivalent to Independence Day (July 4th), which all Americans observe in celebration of the United States gaining independence from Great Britain. Most Americans believe that Abraham Lincoln freed the slaves with a stroke of his pen in 1863. Even though the Emancipation Proclamation went into effect on January 1, 1863, slavery continued in some places in America. It was two and a half years later, on June 19, 1865, that Union soldiers marched into Galveston, Texas, announced the end of the Civil War, and read aloud a general order freeing the quarter-million slaves residing in the state. It is likely that none of the slaves in Texas had any idea that they had actually been freed more than two years before. For those who were still enslaved, it was truly a day of emancipation. That day has become known as Juneteenth Day, a day of celebration for many African Americans. Currently, more than half of states in the U.S. acknowledge Juneteenth in some form, usually on the third Saturday of June. Juneteenth Day is celebrated via cookouts, barbecues, picnics, workplace lunches, neighborhood block parties, community fundraising events, baseball games, displays in city buildings, and essays or artwork competitions for youngsters.

Kwanzaa

Kwanzaa is observed from December 26th to January 1st each year. Some might believe that Kwanzaa is Christmas for African Americans. But Kwanzaa is not a substitute for Christmas. Kwanzaa consists of seven days of celebration featuring candle-lightings and ceremonies and culminating with food and gifts. It was created by Ron Karenga in 1966 as a celebration to give African Americans an opportunity to celebrate themselves and their history. Kwanzaa was established to help African Americans reconnect with their African cultural and historical heritage by uniting in meditation and study of African traditions and common principles. Many Christian African Americans celebrate Kwanzaa and Christmas both. Each of the seven days of Kwanzaa is dedicated to one of the following principles of African culture: unity (*umoja*), self-determination (*kujichagulia*), collective work and responsibility (*ujima*), cooperative economics (*ujamaa*), purpose (*nia*), creativity (*kuumba*), and faith (*imani*) (McClester 1990; Asante & Mattson 1991).

It is difficult to determine the number of African Americans who celebrate Kwanzaa. Estimates range into the millions. In his 2004 Presidential Kwanzaa Message, George W. Bush remarked that while observing Kwanzaa, millions of African Americans and people of African descent gather to celebrate their heritage and ancestry. Kwanzaa celebrations provide an opportunity to focus on the importance of family, community, and history and to reflect on the seven principles of African culture. Kwanzaa is celebrated in homes and institutions throughout America, with speakers, prayers, special programs, and the like.

Martin Luther King, Jr. Day

Dr. Martin Luther King, Jr. is one of the most influential people in American history. Dr. King was the chief spokesman for nonviolent activism in the civil rights movement, which successfully protested racial discrimination in America. Dr. King was assassinated in 1968 at the Lorraine Motel in Memphis, Tennessee. The motel is now the site of the National Civil Rights Museum. In 1968, Representative John Conyers (D-Michigan) introduced legislation for a federal holiday to commemorate Dr. King. In 1983, Congress passed the legislation, and subsequently President Ronald Reagan signed it, creating Martin Luther King, Jr. Day as a federal holiday in America (Martin Luther King, Jr. Day 2012.)

Martin Luther King, Jr. Day is observed on the third Monday of January each year (Chase's 2011), around King's birthday, January 15th. It is one of four United States federal holidays to commemorate an individual person. Martin Luther King's birthday is celebrated with parades, school closings, speeches, special programs, movies, prayers, and so on. It is a day to promote equal rights for all Americans and to remember the work of Dr. King in the struggle against racial segregation and discrimination.

Conclusion

This section has addressed selected demographic data, significant historical information, general cultural group information and basic treatment implications, and holidays and celebrations which may hold prominence with some African Americans. Although this may not provide complete insight to all African Americans, it may be used as a tool for better understanding this cultural group in relation to recreation therapy. How can recreation therapists use the knowledge of these celebrations in recreation therapy practice? Recreation therapists can and should use their creativity and expertise, possibly incorporating these dates and events in websites, bulletin boards, discussions, special events, food, clothing, newsletters, and so on for patients and for their organizations.

References

Asante, M., & Mattson, M. 1991. *Historical and Cultural Atlas of African Americans.* New York: Macmillan Publishing Company.

Bell, D. 2004. *Silent Covenants: Brown v. Board of Education and the Unfulfilled Hopes for Racial Reform.* New York: Oxford University Press.

Black History Month. 2102. *Black History Month.* Retrieved July 6, 2012, from www.history.com/topics/black-history-month.

Butler, J. 1992. Of Kindred Minds: The Ties that Bind. In *Cultural Competence for Evaluators: A Guide for Alcohol and Other Drug Abuse Prevention Practitioners Working with Ethnic/Racial Communities,* edited by M. Orlandi. Rockville, MD: U.S. Department of Health and Human Services.

Chase's Calendar of Events 2011. 2011. New York: McGraw-Hill Companies.

Chideya, F. 1995. *Don't Believe the Hype: Fighting Cultural Misinformation about African Americans.* New York: Plume.

Collins, P. H. 2005. *Black Sexual Politics: African Americans, Gender, and the New Racism.* New York: Routledge Publishing.

D'Souza, D. 1995. *The End of Racism.* New York: The Free Press.

Duke, L. 1991. Race Relations are Worsening. In *Racism in America: Opposing Views,* edited by D. Bender & B. Leone, 17-20. San Diego, CA: Greenhaven Press, Inc.

Elder, L. 2000. *The Ten Things You Can't Say in America.* New York: St. Martin's Press.

Holland, J. 2002. *Black Recreation: A Historical Perspective.* Chicago, IL: Burnham, Inc.

Heilemann, J. & Halperin, M. 2010. *The Game Change: Obama and the Clintons, McCain and Palin, and the Race of a Lifetime.* New York: Harper Collins.

Juneteenth Day. 2012. Worldwide Celebration. Retrieved July 5, 2012, from www.Juneteenth.com.

Manning, M. 1991. *Race, Reform, and Rebellion: The Second Reconstruction in Black America, 1945-1990* (2nd ed.). Jackson, MS: University of Mississippi Press.

Marable, M. 1991. Blacks Should Emphasize their Ethnicity. In *Racism in America: Opposing Views,* edited by D. Bender & B. Leone, 175-183. San Diego, CA: Greenhaven Press, Inc.

Martin Luther King Day. 2012. *Martin Luther King Day in the United States.* Retrieved July 5, 2012, from www.timeanddate.com/holidays/us/martin-luther-king-day.

McClester, C. 1990. *Kwanzaa: Everything You Always Wanted to Know but Didn't Know Where to Ask.* New York: Gumbs & Thomas Publishers.

McNeil, J., Ed. 2002. *Be Safe: A Cultural Competency Model for African Americans.* Howard University, Washington, DC: National Minority AIDS Education and Training Center.

Parker, J. A. 1991. The Rising Black Middle Class Proves Racism is in Decline. In *Racism in America: Opposing Views*, edited by D. Bender & B. Leone, 93-99. San Diego, CA: Greenhaven Press, Inc.

Rastogl, S., Johnson, T., Hoeffel, E., & Drewery, M. 2011. *The Black Population: 2010. 2010 Census Briefs.* Retrieved from www.census.gov/prod/cen2010/briefs/c2010-br-06.pfd on June 18, 2012.

Rowan, C. 1993. *Dream Makers, Dream Breakers: The World of Justice Thurgood Marshall.* Boston, MA: Little, Brown and Company.

Thirteenth Amendment to the U.S. Constitution. 2012. *Primary Documents in American History.* Retrieved from http://www.loc/rr/program/bib/ourdocs/13thamendment.html on June 13, 2012.

U.S. Census Bureau. 2010 Current Population Survey, Annual Social and Economic Supplement.

Wiener, J. 1991. Racism in Higher Education is a Serious Problem. In *Racism in America: Opposing Views*, edited by D. Bender & B. Leone, 54-61. San Diego, CA: Greenhaven Press, Inc.

Wright, E. M. 2001. Substance Abuse in African American Communities. In *Ethnocultural Factors in Substance Abuse Treatment,* edited by S. L. A. Straussner, 31-51. New York: The Guilford Press.

7. Chinese Americans

Immigrants from around the world have entered the U.S. in increasing numbers, often joining their cultural peers in tight ethnic communities. Although currently residing in America, many immigrants have maintained several of their native customs, including languages, foods, holidays, celebrations, traditions, beliefs, values, clothing styles, healthcare issues, societal issues, and recreation and leisure activities. Many of these customs are passed from generation to generation.

Asian Americans are one such group. Immigrants from Asia have passed Hispanics as the number one new immigrant group in the United States, probably due to tougher immigration laws and better U.S. border patrolling. Asian Americans are a diverse group, encompassing individuals from a number of countries. The largest Asian countries include China, Japan, Vietnam, the Philippines, and Taiwan. The cultural differences among peoples from these countries can be significant. As a result, when considering individuals even within one country, there might be significant variance in cultural customs and beliefs. To categorize all Asian Americans — or any other cultural group — as a single entity can be problematic. With this in mind, this chapter will focus on Chinese Americans. Attention will be devoted to general demographic data, important historical information, cultural characteristics and their treatment implications, selected holidays, celebrations, and the recreation of Chinese Americans.

Chinese Americans are U.S. citizens who trace their ancestry to China. Many Chinese Americans maintain strong ties to traditional Chinese customs. The Chinese were the first Asian immigrant group to arrive in the U.S. in large numbers. Today they are the largest Asian

American ethnic group, accounting for about 22% of the Asian American population and about 1.2% of the U.S. population. There are now more than 3.5 million Chinese Americans. Although residing throughout the U.S. (55% live in the South, 9.8% live in the West, 8.9% reside in the Midwest, and 26.4% make their homes in the Northeast), the areas most densely populated with Chinese Americans are along the coast of California, Hawaii, the northeast U.S., the state of Washington, and the western U.S. (Hoeffel et al. 2012).

Chinese Americans are included in virtually all aspects of American life, including athletics, academia, elected offices, entrepreneurial enterprise, and military service. Though other cultural groups may have rather harsh and unfavorable stereotypes attached to them, Chinese Americans often receive a more favorable set of stereotypes. They have often been called the "model minority" because they have tended to assimilate more quickly into American society. Another stereotype of Chinese Americans is that they are proficient in math and science, perhaps because many Chinese who immigrate to the U.S. are educated; many arrive with at least a bachelor's degree, giving the impression of a more intelligent ethnic group. Other stereotypes include being proficient in the martial arts, women being subservient to men, men being antifeminist, and being traditional — that the Chinese culture is basically the same as it was long ago, ancient and mysterious.

Some Important Historical Dates for Chinese Americans

Since the mid-eighteenth century, numerous Chinese have left China. The immigrants left for many reasons, including natural disasters, political shifts in power, and potential economic opportunities offered elsewhere. The beginning of Chinese immigration to America primarily began in Hawaii in the late 1700s. However, most Chinese immigrated to the United States during three distinct time periods: the 1800s, the 1950s, and currently (Campbell & Chang 1981). Many Chinese initially came to America as workers on sugar cane plantations (May Lai 2001).

In the mid 1800s, the Chinese came to the mainland U.S. because they wanted to make a better life for their families through mining or by working on the Transcontinental Railroad. Many hoped to return to mainland China. At that time, some Chinese referred to the U.S. as the "Gold Mountain" due to the California gold rush of the 1800s. Initially, the Chinese were accepted in America because they worked in many laborious jobs for lower pay than Americans would accept. The Chinese played a significant part of laying the economic foundation of the American West with their work on the Transcontinental Railroad. However, in 1882 the Chinese Exclusion Act was established, barring Chinese laborers and their families from entering the country and becoming naturalized citizens. Only Chinese who were travelers, merchants, teachers, students, and those who were born in the U.S. were allowed in the country. This is the only time in U.S. history that America barred a specific ethnic group from entering the nation (Tan 1987). However, during World War I, China became a U.S. ally, and the ban was removed in 1943 with the signing of the Magnuson Act. Since then, the U.S. has allowed the Chinese to immigrate into America.

Chinese American Culture and Customs

In order to become U.S. citizens, Chinese people must be born in America or they must be naturalized citizens. The Chinese government does not believe in dual citizenship, so if an individual becomes an American citizen, their Chinese citizenship is considered renounced. Chinese Americans born in America are sometimes referred to as "ABCs," or "American-Born Chinese." Most ABCs assimilate into American culture relatively easily and are less likely to speak Chinese, even if they learned Chinese while growing up in a Chinese American household. Many ABCs have difficulty reading or writing in Chinese and tend to assimilate more quickly in non-urban, heavily populated areas than they do in other areas with more Chinese Americans. This may be due to the desire of those living in the areas with the densest population of Chinese to maintain traditional Chinese customs.

Many traditional Chinese customs in America are maintained, in part, due to communities referred to as Chinatowns. Chinatowns in U.S. cities like New York, San Francisco, and Chicago have provided strong community support for maintaining traditional Chinese culture. Many of these communities are quite sizeable. For example, the Chinatown in New York City has an estimated 150,000 residents, mostly Chinese American (Waxman 2011). These communities contain all of the amenities found in many cities in China, like groceries, clothing, churches, social organizations, books, magazines, and newspapers. However, recently more Chinese Americans are opting to live in non-Chinese urban areas, where there is more contact with other Americans.

Traditionally, the Chinese have a male-dominated family structure with the father or oldest son having the primary decision-making role. Ideally, the extended family (the father, his parents, the sons, and their families) live in the same household. Traditional Chinese culture holds that family members are expected to adhere to the decisions of the father or oldest sons. In addition, Confucianism is a religion of many Chinese, and Confucianism values include being reverent and obedient to elders and men. As a result, economic and social inequality for women continues in China (Turkington 1999) and might be observed in some Chinese Americans. Raising children is considered the mother's responsibility and children are closely supervised. Cultural conformity is emphasized and children are controlled through principles of guilt and shame if they are disobedient.

Recreation therapists may notice that Chinese American clients/patients may prefer to defer to their elders or to the male heads of their households in determining goals and directions of their treatment.

Many individuals of Chinese ancestry have been taught to be restrained in their demeanor; it is customary for the Chinese to conduct themselves with control. A traditional Chinese value is quietness, and many Chinese try to refrain from loud, boisterous speech and actions

(Kraemer 2006). Consequently, many people of Chinese descent speak in a low to moderate voice. A person with a raised voice may be interpreted as losing control and expressing anger. To many Chinese, Americans are considered loud.

The recreation therapist may need to consider his/her voice tone when interacting with some Chinese Americans. A recreation therapist's loudness may be misinterpreted by the client due to cultural differences.

In public, Chinese Americans may not display many emotions and may limit the use of their body movements. As a result, they might be viewed by others as cold and emotionless, even though a variety of emotions are evident when they interact with their family and friends. However, some may narrow their eyes as an expression of frustration or anger with others who are less close to them (Lowenstein 1995). In attempting to maintain restraint, Chinese Americans may use less eye contact than other Americans do. Direct eye contact may be viewed as rude, so Chinese Americans may look to the side when conversing with professionals.

Recreation therapists may view lack of eye contact as a lack of confidence, whereas the client may view the lack of eye contact as being courteous to others. In the case of some Chinese Americans, this may lead to an improper client evaluation on the part of the recreation therapist.

Another traditional Chinese value is humility (Turkington 1999). Chinese culture maintains that boasting is a rude trait. Recreation therapists may earn more respect from the client by being more modest in their interactions.

As a recreation therapist, it is important to be professional yet restrain from bragging or boasting about credentials, facilities, experiences, and so on when working with someone of Chinese descent.

Because of traditional Chinese values, some Chinese Americans might feel they are disturbing a person of authority if they ask too many questions. As a result, some may suppress their true feelings and remain quiet and polite, even appearing timid.

It is important for the recreation therapist to accurately interpret a client's nonverbal behaviors while analyzing their cultural meaning, and to encourage the client to verbalize concerns.

When there are problems communicating, Chinese Americans may experience feelings of shame and embarrassment. When this happens, many Chinese Americans might repeatedly apologize for inconveniencing the person they are communicating with for their own inadequate language ability.

It is important for the therapeutic recreation specialist to interpret these actions within the context of the Chinese culture and not as an indicator of personal weakness.

Harmony is also important in Chinese culture. Chinese Americans may attempt to avoid conflict and maintain pleasant relationships by not disagreeing or criticizing another person's point of view. To avoid confrontation, the word "no" is seldom used. Consequently, a "yes" when responding to a professional may actually mean a "no" or perhaps a "maybe."

The recreation therapist needs to carefully evaluate client responses. For example, a Chinese person may respond with "yes" when asked if they understand something, even if they do not. Such an admission may cause the person to "lose face." If the therapeutic recreation specialist has concerns regarding an individual's response or interpretation, it might be helpful to have the person repeat the concept or demonstrate the skill or activity.

Along with the concepts of harmony and respect, some Chinese Americans are reluctant to ask the therapist questions about their care and treatment (Kraemer 2006). Some may feel they are troubling or bothering the therapist if they ask too many questions, so they may keep quiet and not indicate their actual feelings.

It's important that the therapeutic recreation specialist accurately assess nonverbal behaviors while encouraging the patient/client to verbalize their concerns and interpretations.

On a personal note: as a professor, I recall a particularly quiet Chinese student in one of my classes some time ago. As a class requirement, all students made a twenty-minute presentation in class. Weeks before her presentation, I inadvertently met her in a hallway, and knowing she was very quiet and reserved, I encouraged her to speak with increased volume and self-assurance during her presentation. My intent was not to have her disrespect her culture. Wanting her presentation to be successful and acknowledging that the majority of her classmates were Americans (who would be peer-evaluating her presentation), I wanted her knowledge of the material to be her peers' focus, not her lack of assertiveness. She assured me she would be assertive. Nevertheless, the student was not much more assertive during her actual presentation. In retrospect, after observing the same student in different social and academic situations, I couldn't determine if her lack of assertiveness was due to traditional Chinese customs or if it was due to her individual personality.

It is important to acknowledge that "saving face" is a significant Chinese value. If one person embarrasses another, it could have a detrimental impact on their relationship (Rickenbacher 2008). When one loses face, one may lose the respect of another. As an example, a person who loses their temper in public may lose face. Or if someone rejects an offer to participate in a leisure or play activity because they have a headache, they may lose face because they're not available. To prevent this, it may be appropriate to apologize for not accepting the invitation while proposing an alternative solution that is acceptable to all parties.

The recreation therapist should be careful to avoid asking questions or making requests that could cause unnecessary embarrassment to the client, especially when attempting to develop rapport with a client.

Developing rapport is important in any relationship. Important to consider when developing rapport are the greetings used between individuals. Therefore, it is important to understand typical greetings in Chinese culture. It is acceptable in American culture to initially greet someone with a handshake (and sometimes a pat on the arm or back when departing.)

The recreation therapist needs to be cognizant that customarily the Chinese may not like to be touched by strangers (Kraemer 2006).

As relationships in Chinese American and non-Chinese American culture continue to develop positively, more physical contact is acceptable. Both handshakes and slight nods of the head are acceptable greetings; nevertheless, a slight nod is more customary and appropriate in Chinese American culture when greeting someone (Rickenbacher 2008). As rapport grows, conversations will expand. As conversations expand, American culture allows people to be somewhat animated in gesturing to aid in getting points or ideas across to another person. Chinese American culture usually does not do this.

Recreation therapists should not use too much excessive hand gesturing and exciting or dramatic facial expressions while talking, as it is customary for Chinese not to use their hands while speaking. Chinese people might become annoyed or distracted by others who are more animated during conversations (Rickenbacher 2008).

Furthermore, when initially meeting a Chinese client, consider that calling a person by any name other than their family name is considered impolite. Customarily, the family name is stated first and then the given name follows. For example, if the individual's family name is Wu and the given name is Yi-Chun, then the proper form of address is Wu Yi-Chun.

Recreation therapists should address people by their title, whole name, or by their family name. It is appropriate to state Mr., Ms., Mrs., or Miss, in addition to their surname. Recreation therapists should ask the client for their preferred name during the initial interview. Because many Americans have trouble pronouncing Chinese names, many Chinese choose to adopt an English or American name in order to address this communication barrier.

The main languages that Chinese Americans speak are English and two dialects of Chinese: Mandarin and Cantonese. Standard Chinese is Mandarin and often referred to as "the common language." It is, in fact, the most commonly spoken language in China (Blacharski 2008). However, in certain cities like Hong Kong and in southern China, Cantonese is the preferred language.

Chinese Americans may have a great deal of their culture based on religion, superstition, education, and philosophy. Religion is probably one of the most visible areas of Chinese culture we notice today. A basic understanding of the most common religions of people of Chinese ancestry will provide knowledge of Chinese American culture. The more popular religions are Buddhism, Confucianism, and Taoism. The following briefly explains some important concepts of these religions.

Buddhism

Buddhism is the largest organized faith among Chinese Americans, and China is believed to have the most Buddhist followers in the world. Buddhism is a religion and philosophy encompassing traditions, beliefs, and practices largely based on teachings attributed to Siddhartha Gautama (the founder of Buddhism), commonly known as the Buddha. Legend has it that Gautama led a wasteful life through early adulthood, enjoying the privileges of his social caste. In time he became bored with indulgences of royal life, and Gautama wandered the world in search of understanding. Eventually, Gautama was convinced that suffering lay at the end of all existence. He renounced his common title and became a monk, depriving himself of worldly possessions, hoping to comprehend the truth of the world around him. Following his enlightenment, Gautama became known as the Buddha, meaning the "Enlightened One."

Karma is a key concept of Buddhism. Contrary to what is accepted in contemporary society, the Buddhist interpretation of karma does not refer to a preordained fate. Rather, karma refers to the results of good or bad actions people take during their lifetime. Good actions, which involve the absence of bad actions — or actual positive acts such as generosity, righteousness, and meditation — bring about happiness in the long run. Bad actions, such as lying, stealing, or killing, bring about unhappiness in the long run. The weight that actions carry is determined by the following conditions: frequency, repetition; determination, and intention. Especially bad are actions performed without regret, actions against extraordinary people, and actions toward those who have helped you in the past (Braswell 1994).

Confucianism

Confucianism is concerned with principles of good conduct, practical wisdom, and proper social relationships. Confucianism is a Chinese ethical and philosophical system developed from the teachings of the Chinese philosopher Confucius. It is a complex system of moral, social, political, philosophical, and quasi-religious thought that has had tremendous influence on the culture and history of East Asia. The basic teachings of Confucianism stress the importance of moral development of the individual so that the state can be governed by moral virtue rather than by coercive laws. Confucianism stresses moral and political ideas. It emphasizes respect for ancestors and government authority and teaches that rulers must govern according to high moral standards.

Confucianism is not a clear-cut belief system in the same way Christianity, Islam, or Judaism are. It does not answer questions about

God and the afterlife. The heart of the Confucian teaching is "morality." Confucianism teaches that people should not do to others things they would not want done to themselves. Confucian philosophy seeks a harmonious society not dependent on feudal or financial merit, but instead based on the ultimate goodness and moral equality of all mankind (Braswell 1994).

Taoism

Taoism refers to the ways of ultimate reality, or the ways of the universe. In other words, Taoism refers to the way people should order their lives and keep them in line with the natural order of the universe. Taoists are indifferent towards things such as rank and excessive luxuries. Taoism is based on the teachings of the Tao Te Ching, written in the sixth century BC in China. Its emphasis on spiritual harmony within the individual complements Confucianism's focus on social duty.

Taoism teaches that everyone should try to achieve two goals: happiness and immortality. To help people to achieve these goals, Taoism offers prayer, magic, special diets, breath control, meditation, and recitation of scriptures. Taoists also believe in astrology, fortune-telling, witchcraft, and communication with the spirits of the dead. Taoists worship more deities than do the followers of almost any other religion. Some deities are ancestors, and others are the spirits of well-known people.

Taoism is based on the idea that behind all material things and all the change in the world lies one fundamental, universal principle: "the Way," or in Chinese, "Tao." This principle gives rise to all existence and governs everything. The purpose of human life is to live according to the Tao, which requires passivity, calmness, non-striving, humility, and lack of planning, for to plan is to go against the Tao (Braswell 1994).

In summary, the concepts of tranquility, calmness, moral development, harmony, and respect are important concepts of traditional Chinese culture and are seen particularly when looking at these common religions.

Holidays, Celebrations, and Recreation

China has several legal holidays each year. Following are five of these holidays and celebrations that may be important to Chinese Americans.

Chinese New Year (Spring Festival)

The Chinese New Year (Spring Festival) is a very special holiday for people of Chinese descent. It is celebrated between January 20th and February 20th. Chinese New Year is China's largest family holiday (Shui & Thompson 1999), celebrated in Chinese communities all over the world (Moehn 2000). Tradition maintains that the event celebrates the death of the old year and the birth of the new year. In China, the Chinese may make preparations, sometimes a month in advance, and many people will take a week off work to prepare for the festivities. The preparation period is often referred to as Little New Year, when parties are arranged to celebrate the day. Chinese legend has it that in ancient times, Buddha asked all the animals to meet him on Chinese New Year. Twelve came: rat, ox, tiger, rabbit, dragon, snake, horse, ram, monkey, rooster, dog, and pig. The Buddha named a year after each one and proclaimed that the people born in each animal's year would have some of that animal's personality.

In preparation for the Chinese New Year, families traditionally give their home a thorough cleaning, hoping to sweep away any of the family's ill-fortune and make way for the arrival of good luck. In China, people may also give their doors and windowpanes a new painting, usually red. Red symbolizes fire, which according to legend can drive away bad luck. They decorate doors and windows with paper cutouts, adhering to the popular themes of happiness, wealth, longevity, and satisfactory marriage and children. Paintings of the same themes are hung inside the homes.

The eve of the Chinese New Year is also given attention. Supper is a feast, with family members coming together. After the final meal of the day, the family stays up late into the night playing cards, games, or watching TV programs dedicated to the occasion. It is also a tradition to keep lights on in the house throughout the night. People wear red clothes, decorate with poems on red paper, and give children "lucky money" in red envelopes, which they open the next morning (again the color red symbolizes luck and is believed to drive away bad luck). At midnight, fireworks light up the sky as everyone's excitement reaches its peak. The fireworks that shower the festivities are rooted in a similar ancient custom. Long ago, people in China lit bamboo stalks, believing that the crackling flames would frighten evil spirits.

On New Year's Day, children greet their parents and receive their presents of cash wrapped up in red paper packages. Then the family continues the day by going door to door and greeting relatives and neighbors. The Chinese New Year tradition is a great way to reconcile while forgetting all old grudges. There is a sense of warmth and friendliness in the air.

Custom has it that new clothes are bought, especially for children. Red scrolls with complimentary poetic memos are posted in homes. The Chinese character *Fu* is pasted on the center of doors, and paper-cut pictures adorn windows. *Fu* in Chinese means good luck or happiness. By pasting this character on the center of the door, people display the hope to be happy. Currently, people like to paste it backward, for this means Fu has come. The Chinese also set off firecrackers, which means bidding farewell to the past year and welcoming the New Year (Spring Festival 2012; Chinese Festivals 2012).

During and several days following Chinese New Year's Day, people visit each other and exchange gifts. Today, many Chinese-American neighborhood associations host banquets and other New Year events. The New Year atmosphere is brought to an end fifteen days later when the Festival of Lanterns starts. The Lantern Festival marks the end of the Chinese New Year season and afterwards individuals resume their typical daily routines.

The Chinese Lantern Festival

The Chinese Lantern Festival is celebrated on the last day of the traditional Chinese New Year. The Lantern Festival marks the end of the series of celebrations starting from the Chinese New Year. This is first significant feast after the Spring Festival.

In China, during the Lantern Festival thousands of lanterns are hung in the streets and children go out at night carrying bright lanterns (Moehn 2000). The lanterns are embroidered with many designs; sometimes they're even works of art painted with birds, animals, flowers, zodiac signs, and scenes from legend and history. People hang glowing lanterns in temples or carry the lanterns to evening parades under the light of the full moon. The lanterns symbolize good luck and hope (Lantern Festival 2012).

In many areas in China, the highlight of the lantern festival is the dragon dance. The dragon might stretch a hundred feet long and is typically made of silk, paper, and bamboo. Traditionally, the dragon is held up by young men who dance as they guide the colorful beast through the streets. The dragon dance typically takes place in weekend celebrations. In the U.S., many Chinese-American communities have become somewhat Americanized; traditional American parade elements are sometimes included, such as marching bands and floats. Other popular activities include eating sweet rice dumplings served in a sugary soup, and guessing lantern riddles, which are often messages of love intended for others.

Dragon Boat Festival

The Dragon Boat Festival is typically celebrated in May or June (Shui & Thompson 1999). The exact date will vary from year to year. The festival has been held annually for more than 2,000 years and is notable for its educational influence. The festival commemorates the Chinese patriotic poet Qu Yang (340-278 BC) and is a chance for Chinese people to build their bodies and dispel diseases. It is a fun holiday even though it commemorates the sad tale of Qu Yuan. Legend has it that Qu Yuan drowned himself in a river rather than see his country occupied and conquered by a corrupt government. Upon hearing of Qu Yuan's death, all the local people were in great distress. Local fishermen searched for his body by sailing their boats down the river, and other people threw food into the river to attract the fish and other animals so they would not destroy Qu Yuan's body. Many people imitate these acts even today to show their respect for this great patriotic poet.

Activities of the Dragon Boat Festival generally include dragon boat racing, eating *zongzi* (pyramid-shaped dumplings with sticky rice wrapped in reed or bamboo leaves), wearing perfume pouches, tying five-color silk threads, and hanging special plants on the doors of homes. Zongzi are sometimes given as gifts when people visit relatives and friends during the festival (Shui & Thompson 1999; Moehn 2000).

Dragon boats are long, narrow boats elaborately decorated with a painted dragon head at the front. Dragon boat races consist of a team of people in boats rowing to cross a finish line first. Similar to rowing races in the U.S., one team member sits at the front of the boat beating a drum in order to maintain morale and ensure rowers keep in time with one another. The boats are shaped like the traditional Chinese dragon. Legend holds that the race originated from the idea of the people who rowed their boats to save Qu Yuan after he threw himself in the river. It is said that the winning team will bring a good harvest and happy life to the people of their village.

Another Dragon Boat custom is wearing a perfume pouch, which protects children from evil. So on this day, children decorate their clothes with differently fragranced pouches made of colorful silk cloth strung with five-color silk thread. It is also customary to tie five-color silk thread to a child's wrists, ankles, and neck. The five-color thread holds special significance in China; it is thought to contain magical and healing properties. Children are not permitted to speak while their parents tie the five-color thread for them. They are also not allowed to remove it until a specified time. Traditionally, after the first summer rainfall, the children can throw the thread into the river. This is thought to protect the children from plague and diseases.

The festival is held in late spring or early summer, when diseases are most prevalent, so people clean their houses and put special plants on the tops of doors in their homes to discourage disease. It is thought that the stems and leaves discharge a special aroma that can dispel mosquitoes and flies and purify the air, so this custom is understandably popular.

Mid-Autumn Festival

The Mid-Autumn Festival is also known as the Moon Festival because this the time of the year the moon is at its fullest. This festival is also a traditional holiday for family members and lovers.

In celebration, family members gather to appreciate the bright full moon, eat moon cakes at night, express strong desires for peaceful and happy homes, and reminisce about family members who live far away who will also be gazing up at the moon. A moon cake is round, and it symbolizes the reunion of a family. So it is easy to understand how eating moon cakes under the round moon can inspire thoughts of distant relatives. Today, people present the moon cakes to relatives and friends to demonstrate that they wish them a long and happy life (Chinavoc 2007).

Conclusion

This section has addressed demographic data, significant historical information, general cultural group information, basic treatment implications, and holidays and celebrations of Chinese Americans. Although the information will not provide complete insight to all Chinese Americans, it may be used as a basic tool for better understanding this cultural group in regards to recreation therapy service delivery.

As is noted from the cultural customs mentioned for people of Chinese descent (as it is with all racial or ethnic groups), identifying, describing, and adequately understanding the numerous cultural customs associated with or important to that group can be a significant step toward cultural competence.

References

Blacharski, D. 2008. *The Savvy Business Traveler's Guide to Customs and Practices in Other Countries: The Do's and Don'ts to Impress Your Host and Make the Sale.* Ocala, FL: Atlantic Publishing Group.

Braswell, B. 1994. *Understanding World Religions.* Nashville, TN: Broadman & Holman Publishers.

Campbell, T. & Chang, B. 1981. Health Care of the Chinese in America. In *Transcultural Health Care,* edited by G. Henderson & M. Primeaux, 162-171. Reading, MA: Addison-Wesley.

Chinavoc. 2007. Mid-Autumn festival. Retrieved June 10, 2012, from www.chinavoc.com/festivals/Midautum.htm.

Chinese Festivals. 2012. Traditional Chinese Festivals. Retrieved June 15, 2012, from www.china.cn/English/features/Festivals/78322.htm.

Hoeffel, E., Rastogl, S., Kim, M., & Shahid, H. 2012. The Asian Population: 2010. 2010 Census Briefs. Retrieved from www.census.gov/prod/cen2010/briefs/c2010-br-11.pfd on July 2, 2012.

Kraemer, T. 2006. Cultural Considerations for the Chinese Culture. In *Developing Cultural Competence in Physical Therapy Practice,* edited by J. B. Lattanzi & L. D. Purnell, 197-207. Philadelphia, PA: F. A. Davis Company.

Lantern Festival. 2012. Lantern Festival. Retrieved July 5, 2012, from www.travelchinaguide.com/essentail/holidays/lantern.htm.

Lowenstein, A. & Glandville, C. 1995. Cultural Diversity and Conflict in the Heath Care Workplace. *Nursing Economics 13*: 203-209.

May Lai, T. 2001. Ethnocultural Background and Substance Abuse Treatment of Chinese Americans. In *Ethnocultural Factors in Substance Abuse Treatment,* edited by S. L. A. Straussner, 345-367. New York: The Guilford Press.

Moehn, H. 2000. *World Holidays: A Watts Guide for Children.* Danbury, CT: Grolier Publishing.

Rickenbacher, C. A. 2008. *Be on Your Cultural Best: How to Avoid Social and Professional Faux Pas When Dining, Traveling, Conversing, and Entertaining.* Bel Air, CA: Worlds of Wonder Publishing.

Shui, A. & Thompson, S. 1999. *China: Foods and Festivals*. Austin, TX: Steck-Vaughn Company.

Spring Festival. 2012. Spring Festival of China. Retrieved July 5, 2012, from www.travelchinaguide.com/essential/holidays/spring-festival.htm.

Tan, T. T. 1987. *Your Chinese Roots*. Union City, CA: Heian.

Turkington, C. 1999. *The Complete Idiot's Guide to Cultural Etiquette*. Indianapolis, IN: Alpha Books.

United States Census Bureau. 2010, March 2. Facts for Features: Asian/Pacific American Heritage Month. Retrieved September 14, 2011, from http://wwwcensus.gov/newsroom/releases/archives/facts_for_features_speci al_editions/cb10-f07.html.

Waxman, S. 2011. The History of New York's Chinatown. Retrieved from http://www.ny.com/articles/chinatown.html. on July 5 2012.

8. *Japanese Americans*

Japanese Americans are U.S. citizens who trace their ancestry to Japan. According to the 2010 census, approximately 1,304,286 Japanese Americans live in the U.S. (Hoeffel et al. 2012). Japanese Americans are the third-largest Asian American ethnic group in the United States. The majority of Japanese Americans live in California, Oregon, Washington, Hawaii, and New York; however, several other states have significant populations as well. Thousands of new immigrants come to the U.S. each year from Japan, but the Japanese American population remains relatively stable because many elderly Japanese return to Japan later in their lives.

Some Important Historical Dates for Japanese Americans

Prior to the Meiji Restoration (before 1868), Japan was in virtual isolation from the rest of the world and operated in a feudalistic capacity. The Meiji ("Enlightened Rule") Period refers to the 45-year reign of the Meiji Emperor, from 1868 to 1912. During this time period, Japan began its modernization and rose to world-power status. The Meiji Restoration of 1868 ended the 265-year-old feudalistic Tokugawa shogunate. After the death of the Meiji Emperor in 1912, the Taishō Emperor took the throne, thus beginning the Taishō period in Japanese history.

The first significant Japanese immigration to the United States began in 1868, the first year after the Meiji Period. Between 1896 and 1911, more than 400,000 Japanese came to the U.S., primarily to California and Hawaii. Most of the Japanese immigrants came to the U.S. for the same reasons most other immigrants did — to make a better life for themselves and their families. As a relatively young country, the U.S. was constructing its infrastructure, and the railroad industry actively recruited first-generation Japanese, called *issei*, from Hawaii and Japan to work as laborers. To that end, numerous Japanese workers helped construct a number of railroads in the West.

In addition, during the 1880s Japanese Americans worked in various plantation and agricultural jobs to support their families. Eventually they began to sharecrop and lease land while establishing community life in the U.S. As the immigrants began to find successes in their new nation, many whites were threatened by these accomplishments. As a result, the California Alien Land Act of 1913 was established to ban Japanese from purchasing land in the state. The Federal Immigration Act of 1924 banned further immigration from Japan. Nevertheless, the issei were becoming successful economically in California and Hawaii.

After the start of WWII, which began as the result of the Japanese bombing Pearl Harbor, President Franklin Roosevelt issued Executive Order 9066, which mandated that people of Japanese ancestry in the U.S. be forcibly detained in internment camps in America. Approximately 120,000 people of Japanese ancestry were detained in ten inland internment concentration camps in seven states in the U.S.

Internment was based solely on race and ancestry, not political or other activity. Entire families were incarcerated together. Life in internment was harsh. Each family member was allowed to bring only two suitcases of belongings with them to the camps. In the camps, a family was provided one room — no matter the family's size — to live in. The camps were fenced in and patrolled by armed guards. Yet despite the camps' harsh and unsanitary conditions and illegitimate persecution, those who were interned tried to make the most out of their lives while they were imprisoned. They played sports games, published their own newspaper, planted flowers, played music, and completed craft projects. Most of those who were interned stayed at the camps until the end of the war. At the war's end, they left the camps and started to rebuild their lives. However, as a result of their confinement, Japanese Americans lost their homes, jobs, friends, businesses, and monetary savings.

In 1980, Congress created the Commission on Wartime Relocation and Internment of Civilians to investigate internment during World War II. In 1983, the commission found that internment was not justified by military necessity and was based on "race prejudice," war hysteria, and a failure of political leadership. Subsequently the commission recommended an official government apology, redress payments of $20,000 to each of the survivors, and a public education fund to help ensure that this would never happen again. It was not until 1988 that President Ronald Regan signed the Civil Liberties Act of 1988, which apologized for the internment and provided $20,000 to each victim. Despite this history, people of Japanese ancestry have continued to make progress in all aspects of life in America.

Japanese American Culture and Customs

Working with Japanese clients may present challenges to recreation therapists who are unfamiliar with Japanese culture. The Japanese population in the U.S. tends to fall into three categories: descendents of early immigrants, immigrants who arrived after World War II, and visiting business people and their families (Straussner 2001). Each group may have different levels of acculturation into U.S. culture. The largest category is descendents of those who immigrated to the U.S. between 1900 and 1924. Many of these descendents have been in the U.S. for many decades and have become very acculturated into the U.S. Included in the second group are "war brides," wives of American servicemen stationed in Japan after World War II. Many of these unions ended in divorce, and many of the women did not have sufficient time to fully acculturate into U.S. society. Consequently, many may have maintained much of their Japanese culture. The last group, Japanese businessmen and their families, are in the U.S. for shorter periods of time and generally plan to return to Japan after their stays in the U.S. This group is more likely to retain many of their Japanese cultural traditions.

Early Japanese immigrants and others that followed abided by traditional cultural traits of feudal Japan and the more industrialized Meiji Period. These characteristics include a preference of group loyalty over individual desires, maintaining harmony, keeping emotions reserved, delaying gratification, and respect for authority figures (Straussner 2001). The characteristics maintained in social situations and accepted behavior may continue to shape the behavior of current Japanese Americans.

Traditional Japanese take pride in Japanese customs and traditions. As such, those of Japanese ancestry are likely, like those of any cultural heritage, to have pride in their cultural heritage. Additionally, Japanese custom maintains that Japanese should be loyal to Japanese culture. Individuality is not a positive concept in Japanese culture; unity and collectivism are important concepts to keep in mind for those of Japanese descent.

Recreation therapists must be mindful that when working with people of Japanese descent, acknowledging traditional cultural customs, such as a preference for group rather than individual goals, can be an important ingredient to success in relationships with them.

Communication for some traditional Japanese Americans is influenced by the traditional Japanese cultural concepts of *enryo, garman,* and *haji.* Enryo means that one should have self-restraint when interacting with others. Enryo also implies polite hesitation during communication with others. Garman is a concept in which self-control and the ability to endure are important. Haji relates to the concept of shame. Shame is to be seriously avoided, as shame reflects upon family and family name as well as the individual.

As such, recreation therapists may notice that nonverbal communication with Japanese Americans might be quiet and polite, with relatively little direct eye contact.

Greetings might be a focal area to consider when interacting with people of Japanese ancestry. Greetings are very important in Japanese culture, and there may be different ones. Traditionally, greetings begin with a bow or a handshake. Bowing — simply bending half the body from the waist — can go a long way when interacting with people of Japanese descent, helping the therapist better connect with patients. Bowing may express apology and respect. Bowing depth and the duration of the bow may differ depending on the situation and the relationship of the people involved (Blacharski 2008; Turkington 1999).

Recreation therapists might consider starting their interactions with Japanese Americans with a bow as a means of displaying awareness of Japanese culture.

It is important for therapist to establish expert credibility, especially when working with more recent or more traditionally oriented Japanese Americans (Matsuyoushi cited, in Straussner 2001).

In attempting to establish credibility, the recreation therapist might consider mentioning his or her experiences and successes with Japanese people or explaining particular educational training.

Therapists should be aware of how traditional Japanese caregiver-patient interactions may impact their relationship with the client. In Japan, caregiver-patient relationships are influenced by respect for higher status. In this relationship, clients expect the therapist to make rapid diagnoses and provide the client with concrete solutions to their problems (Munakata 1986).

With this possible cultural expectation in mind, the therapeutic recreation specialist may need to educate the client about the general nature of the therapeutic recreation process. The client will need to understand that some solutions are initially recommended, and as assessments and interactions continue, that courses of action may be altered as additional information is gathered, and that patient/client involvement in the recreation therapy process is often encouraged. However, the therapist may need to take a more autocratic approach when working with Japanese Americans. Japanese culture maintains respect and acknowledgement of authority figures. Clients might be inclined to accept treatment goals and interventions with little personal input. Nevertheless, this might present significant challenges, as therapeutic recreation specialists are trained to actively include clients, and often significant others, in their treatment.

It is customary for Japanese to be respectful to elders and authority figures. As in most situations when individuals are very respectful to others, those providing the respect may not indicate their true feelings on a particular issue when suggestions or opinions are provided by those in positions of authority.

Since recreation therapists may be considered authority people by the nature of their professional positions, some Japanese Americans may not provide insights into their true feelings and may look to the professional for solutions.

First and second generation Japanese Americans typically speak Japanese as their first language. While later generations typically learn English first, some might eventually learn how to speak Japanese later in life.

If an interpreter is used (especially if that person is not familiar with the profession), it might be wise for the recreation therapist to meet with the interpreter beforehand and explain general information regarding how recreation therapists interact with clients.

A significant number of Japanese Americans might practice Buddhism, Shintoism, or Christianity. Most Americans are familiar with and practice Christianity, and Buddhism has been described in the previous section on Chinese Americans.

Shintoism

In Shintoism, there is the belief God is in everything. According to Japanese custom, it is believed that the emperor is a descendent of God. Shinto is thought to embrace the following concepts: "the way of the Gods," "the God-like way," or "the way from the Gods." It is a religion of the heart. Shinto is believed to be a natural spiritual force which pervades the lives of the Japanese. Shinto is a creative or formative principle of life. The Shinto principle provides part of the background of Japanese culture, code of ethics, fine arts, family, and national structure. Purity is one of the fundamental virtues of Shinto ethics. There are two aspects: outer or bodily purity, and inner purity or purity of heart. If a man is endowed with true inner purity of heart, he will surely attain God-realization or communion with the divine. Sincerity is also the guiding ethical principle of Shinto.

Holidays, Celebrations, and Recreation

New Year's (shogatsu)

Japanese New Year is one of the most important holidays in Japan. In Japan, many businesses close down from January 1st to January 3rd, and families typically gather to spend these days together. Theoretically, each new year should provide a fresh start, so before January 1st, all current duties are supposed to be completed.

On New Year's Eve Bonenkai (year-forgetting) parties are held with the purpose of leaving the old year's worries and troubles behind. Homes and entranceways are decorated with ornaments made of pine, bamboo, and plum trees, and clothes and houses are thoroughly cleaned. *Toshikoshi* soba (buckwheat noodles), symbolizing longevity, are often served during meals. A more recent custom is watching television music shows featuring many of Japan's most famous singers in spectacular performances.

January 1st is a very auspicious day, as the day is supposed to be full of joy and free of stress and anger. Everything should be clean and people should be free from work responsibilities. Also, it is a tradition to visit a shrine or temple during New Year's Day. On the actual turn of the year, large temple bells are rung at midnight. Various kinds of special dishes are served on New Year's Day, including sweetened rice wine and soup.

Coming of Age (seijin no hi)

The Coming of Age celebration occurs on the second Monday of January. On this day, all young people who turn twenty years old in that year are acknowledged and celebrated, as this is the age considered to be the beginning of adulthood. In Japan, twenty years is the minimum legal age for voting, alcohol consumption, and smoking. In Japan, celebrations are held nationwide in every town with most of the people turning twenty participating and in formal dress. Celebrations might include gatherings and parties.

Doll's Festival (hina matsuri)

Doll's Festival occurs on March 3rd. On this day, families with girls wish their daughters a successful and happy life. During the festival, ornamental dolls are displayed on platforms representing the emperor, empress, their attendants, and musicians in traditional dress of the Heian Period. During the Heian Period, people believed the dolls possessed the power to contain bad spirits.

White Day

Essentially the opposite of Valentine's Day, White Day is celebrated on March 14th. White Day is a day for men to return the favors that they received on Valentine's Day. Men celebrating White Day give presents and chocolates to their girlfriends or wives.

Conclusion

This section has addressed demographic data, significant historical information, general cultural group information, basic treatment implications, and holidays and celebrations of Japanese Americans. Although the information provided will not provide complete insight to all Japanese Americans, it may be used as a basic tool for better understanding this cultural group as it relates to recreation therapy service delivery.

As is noted from the cultural customs previously mentioned for people of Japanese descent (as it is with all racial or ethnic groups), identifying, describing, and adequately understanding cultural customs associated with or important to that group can be a significant step toward cultural competence.

References

Blacharski, D. (2008). *The savvy business traveler's guide to customs and practices in other countries: The do's and don'ts to impress your host and make the sale.* Ocala, FL: Atlantic Publishing Group.

Chin, Frank. 2002. *Born in the USA: A Story of Japanese America, 1889-1947.* Lanham, MD: Rowan and Littlefield.

Commission on Wartime Relocation and Internment of Civilians. 1982. *Personal Justice Denied: Report of the Commission on Wartime Relocation and Internment of Civilians.* Washington, DC: Government Printing Office.

Daniels, Roger. 1962. *The Politics of Prejudice: The Anti-Japanese Movement in California and the Struggle for Japanese Exclusion (2nd ed.).* Berkeley, CA: University of California Press.

Daniels, Roger. 1981. *Concentration Camps, North America: Japanese in the United States and Canada during World War II.* Malabar, FL: R. E. Krieger, Publisher.

Conroy, Hilary & Miyakawa T. Scott, editors. 1972. *East Across the Pacific: Historical and Sociological Studies of Japanese of Immigration and Assimilation.* Ann Arbor, MI: American Bibliographical Center-Clio Press.

Hoeffel, E., Rastogl, S., Kim, M., & Shahid, H. 2012. *The Asian Population: 2010. 2010 Census Briefs.* Retrieved from www.census.gov/prod/cen2010/briefs/c2010-br-11.pfd. Accessed July 2, 2012.

Straussner. S. (2001). Ethnocultural issues in substance abuse treatment. In Strausnner, S. (Ed.) *Ethnocultural Factors in the Treatment of Addictions.* New York. NY: Guilford Press.

Munakata, T. 1986. Japanese Attitudes Towards Mental Health and Mental
    Health Care. In *Japanese Culture and Behavior,* edited by T. S. Lebra & W.
    P. Lebra, 369-378. Honolulu: University of Hawaii Press.
Turkington, C. 1999. *The Complete Idiot's Guide to Cultural Etiquette.*
    Indianapolis, IN: Alpha Books.
Varley, H. Paul. 1997. *Japanese Culture: A Short History (expanded ed.).* New
    York: Praeger Publishers, Inc.

9. Hmong Americans

Hmong Americans are United States citizens who trace their ancestry to China, Laos, Vietnam, and Thailand. The first wave of Hmong entered the United States in the mid-1970s. The total Hmong population in the U.S., according to the 2010 U.S. Census, is approximately 247,595 (Hoeffel et al. 2012). The majority of Hmong live in California, Minnesota, Rhode Island, and Texas (McInnis, Petracchi, & Morgenbesser 1990).

Some Important Historical Dates for Hmong Americans

The Hmong are one of Vietnam's numerous ethnic minority groups, representing three sub-groups: Black Hmong, Green Hmong, and White Hmong (Smolan & Erwitt 1994). The Hmong have always had a rich farming tradition. Working the land and farming might be considered a survival kit for the Hmong; these traditions are deeply embedded in Hmong culture. Traditionally, Hmong families have grown their own vegetables and raised their own animals both to derive income and put food on the table for their families. Most Hmong families do not come from wealthy backgrounds, and many lack a formal education, so the Hmong have often struggled to obtain educationally related jobs requiring higher education in many cities in America. As people from mountainous regions, the Hmong have long depended on themselves and their traditional farming skills for survival.

During the Vietnam War, many Hmong in Laos entered into a secret agreement with the U.S. In 1960, the U.S. Central Intelligence Agency (CIA) sought the support of General Vang Pao (GVP), a famous Hmong general in the Royal Lao Army, in their fight against Vietnamese communists. In return for GVP's backing, the Americans promised arms, training, food, and money for the Hmong during the conflict. At that time, an estimated 500,000 Hmong lived in Laos. The U.S. guaranteed that by helping the U.S. in the war, the Hmong would be given their own land and would be protected by the U.S. government. With high respect for GVP's decision to support the U.S., about 30,000 Hmong fought against the Vietnamese, being paid an average of ten cents per day, with the promise of U.S. government protection. In 1975, the U.S. pulled out of the war in Southeast Asia. An estimated 17,000 Hmong soldiers and 5,000 civilians were killed in the war.

Eventually the communists won the conflict, and the Hmong who had assisted the U.S. were actively persecuted in Laos. Worse, the communists insisted that all Hmong were traitors. The communists then sought to punish and exterminate all Hmong men, women, and children. The Hmong were virtually defenseless as the U.S. pulled its military and financial support out of Laos. Hmong men were slaughtered, Hmong women were raped and killed, and even innocent children were poisoned or killed. Some surrendered to the communists, and the rest were hunted like animals. In order to escape this hunt, many Hmong ran to the jungles of Laos to hide, where many died due to starvation and sickness. Those who had surrendered to the Laotian communists were never heard of again. Many Hmong ran through jungles and swam across the Mekong River to Thailand, where the Thai government had set up refugee camps for the Hmong. Thailand soon became home to those that had escaped death.

Within a few years, many Hmong were granted asylum in the U.S., honoring the promise made by the U.S. The first wave of Hmong refugees came to the U.S. in the mid-1970s, many bringing very few personal possessions. Hmong refugees were either well-educated or farmers with no educational backgrounds. Some Hmong families immigrated to France, Australia, and other countries. In 1980, another 100,000 Hmong fled to Thailand. Some stayed in United Nations camps for up to ten years. In 1995, the Thai refugee camps started closing. Thousands of Hmong were forced to return to Laos, where there were continuing reports of torture and persecution. In 1997, the Hmong were finally recognized in Washington D.C. for their efforts during the Vietnam War (Yang 2012). In 2003, the last refugee camp, Wat Tham Krabak, was closed, and approximately 15,000 Hmong refugees from that camp resettled in the United States (Yang 2012).

An important date the Hmong Americans will never forget is January 6, 2011: the death of General Vang Pao. As mentioned earlier, many Hmong have high respect for GVP. He's considered by many Hmong to be the "king" or the father of the Hmong, and a true hero. When his death was announced, many Hmong did not want to believe it was true. When GVP's funeral was held in California, only those close to him — those who could purchase airline tickets, take time off work, and who were part of the Secret War — had the chance to see GVP for the last time. Many who couldn't make it to GVP's funeral in California participated in local community gatherings to pay homage to GVP and to say their last goodbyes.

Hmong American Culture and Customs

In this section, culture, customs, and other important information about the Hmong are addressed. Treatment implications for recreational therapists working with the Hmong are also addressed. It is important to note that many Hmong cultural traditions have not been written and are passed down through word-of-mouth from generation to generation (Smolan & Erwitt 1994). As such, some Hmong cultural traditions may be difficult for recreation therapists to comprehend. For example, in La Crosse, Wisconsin, in 2013, a Hmong man was charged with threatening a woman who refused to have an abortion. To retaliate, the man said he tampered with the woman's car and rotated her bed. The man asserted that in Hmong culture, these actions could bring bad luck to the woman and her child (Jungen 2013).

Preserving Hmong culture is important to the Hmong, as evidenced by the following quote from Kao-Ly Yang, PhD, (2012) from the foreword of the article *Common Basis and Characteristics of Miao and Hmong Identity* by Zhang Xiao:

> Whatever the countries we may live either in the East, in the Southeast, or in the West, whatever word we may use to call ourselves, either "Miao", "Hmong" (Hmoob), "Mong" (Moob), or "Meo", we all shall remember and cherish our common cultural heritage made of sub cultures and our diverse dialects, and the fragments of our history that we have kept in memory. Whatever good relationship that we may maintain within our community, whatever our ideology beliefs or lifestyle we seek to promote, how acculturated in the Western cultures that we may become, we shall protect and preserve the unity of our ethnic group as a necessity to enhance our kind so that our descendants will have better opportunities to appear and voice as one unique group before the challenges of modern societies

Yang's comments remind us of the importance of the preservation of culture for the Hmong. These comments are especially relevant considering that the Hmong have histories and life experiences in many countries around the world.

The Hmong are culturally motivated to live near their relatives and clansman for support. Historically, the Hmong have preferred to live independently and in peace. Even in a country known for peace and freedom, the Hmong still face challenges in the U.S., and they are often the target of false beliefs and inaccurate misinterpretations, misconceptions, and stereotypes. A common misconception is that the Hmong are Chinese or Japanese due to their physical appearance, skin complexion, and hair color and style. Other misconceptions and misinterpretations include that the Hmong are avid polygamists, or that they're primitive, uncivilized, or brutal — even that Hmong families will sell their daughters into marriage. Still other stereotypes include that Hmong worship chickens and eat their dogs.

It is important for recreation therapists to understand and acknowledge possible misconceptions and stereotypes of the Hmong. Although it is true that some Hmong once had more than one wife or that they sacrificed animals during ceremonial observances, these practices are uncommon for the vast majority of Hmong Americans.

In Laos, Hmong society was semi-nomadic and primarily based on farming. As previously mentioned, farming was a means of survival for the Hmong. When they left Laos and came to the U.S., the Hmong had to adapt to a culture very different from their own. Many Hmong were not used to competing in the urban workforce; most were farmers and had few marketable skills that would lend themselves to higher-level vocations in a more technology-based working world. They also did not have adequate educational backgrounds — most were not able to speak, read, or write in English. Even today some Hmong Americans, especially many of the older Hmong, do not speak English.

It is important for the recreation therapist when working with a client to understand that an interpreter may be needed.

Nevertheless, many Hmong have adapted to American culture rather well and are obtaining degrees from colleges and universities and acquiring professional positions. Some maintain much of the traditional Hmong culture (Mattison, Lo, & Scarseth 1994), but many of the younger Hmong pursue education due to the support of their parents, even as the parents still cling to traditional Hmong beliefs.

In the Hmong language, there are two dialects: White Hmong and Green Hmong (sometimes referred to as Blue Hmong). White Hmong is usually preferred, because the written form of Hmong is closest to the pronunciation of White Hmong language, although neither is considered to be of higher status.

Traditional Hmong social structure is based on clans, which are determined by ancestral lineage and on particular ceremonies they practice. Lineage is usually based on last names. There are about eighteen different Hmong clans with different last names (Culhane-Pera & Xiong 2003). Each clan is divided into sub-clans. Members of these groups are made of many families who may or may not share the same ancestor. Each sub-clan subscribes to a particular religious practice or ritual. Sub-clans are further broken down into families, the most basic unit, consisting of members linked only through bloodline. According to Hmong culture, each level has a selected male leader responsible for making decisions for all family members. At times, specialized secondary leaders, such as religious leaders, can also be selected as decision makers.

Hmong culture mandates the father to be the head of the household. The father makes the decisions for the family, and men tend to have more status and power than women do (Culhane-Pera & Xiong 2003). However, Hmong families do not respect mothers any less than they do fathers — the idea is simply to have one person with the power to make decisions. When the father is absent, the oldest son has the power to make decisions for the family.

Recreation therapists should be aware that a patient/client may defer to the specified "family decision-maker" in making treatment and rehabilitation decisions.

If a family does not have a living father or any male sons, the family may select a respected clan leader to make decisions for them. Traditionally, Hmong mothers nurture and take care of the children and are responsible for maintaining the household. However in families today, it is becoming more common for fathers and mothers to both make decisions. Women are becoming more active outside the household as they attend school, are more actively employed, and take on more leadership roles in their communities.

The Hmong elderly are accorded high respect from family members. Elderly Hmong are typically consulted on important decisions. However, in the U.S. the elderly are less often consulted for their wisdom and are less respected than they were in the past (Culhane-Pera & Xiong 2003). This is understandable; the elders have had a much harder time adjusting to life in America than their children and grandchildren have. Consequently, for older Hmong, learning the English language is difficult, and communicating with outsiders can be a challenge. Even a simple activity like shopping without an interpreter can difficult. Such difficulty in communication may enhance the social isolation of some Hmong. As a result, for many elders, basic survival in America may be disabling. When one considers that many of the elder Hmong may not read, write, or speak English, let alone drive cars, they will depend on their children to get them around and communicate with others on their behalf. This in itself can be disabling.

Traditional Hmong culture considers prolonged direct eye contact to be rude. Also, when speaking, the tone of one's voice should be modulated or controlled and not very animated.

It is important for recreation therapists to understand that even though their clients may not look directly at them during therapist-client interactions, Hmong clients are indeed listening. Direct eye contact is rude in the Hmong culture; therefore, recreation therapists should not misinterpret such behavior as being timid, shy, or non-assertive.

Historically and culturally the Hmong are "presently" time-oriented. Consequently, keeping appointment times may be difficult. It is not uncommon for social events within the Hmong culture to start much later than the stated time.

It may be important for recreation therapists to remind their clients of appointments, especially older Hmong clients.

The Hmong are a very spiritual people. Spirit types include ancestral spirits, house spirits, and natural spirits. Some Hmong wear white clothes and will tie red or white strings on their wrist and necks to keep away spirits who might bring misfortune or sickness. Traditional Hmong of Shamanistic faith might continue such practice beliefs. However, the more modern or acculturated Hmong in America are slowly embracing Christianity as their religious belief. Although both groups believe in worshipping their ancestors and respecting spirits, most beliefs of traditional Hmong and modern Hmong are different. The modern Hmong do not hold rituals or believe in sacrificing animals to worship their ancestors.

It is important for the recreation therapist to acknowledge the client's spiritual view or religious belief. Understanding that individuals are different and come with different beliefs and values will help create a safe and more welcoming environment for the client.

Shamanism

As previously mentioned, the Hmong are culturally a very spiritual people. The traditional religion practiced by Hmong is Shamanism. Although Hmong families are often animists in the United States, Hmong families are slowly embracing Christianity as their new religious view. (Animists hold strong beliefs that spirits inhabit objects and are the causes of many phenomena.) A large number of Christian Hmong families still practice some form of Hmong traditional religion out of respect and homage to their elders and to traditional Hmong cultural customs. Each clan has different variations of traditions and practices passed down through oral practices.

Shamanism comprises a range of beliefs and practices concerned with communication with the spiritual world. Shamans, the spiritual leaders or "medicine men," are viewed as intermediaries or messengers between the natural world and spirit worlds (Mattison, Lo, & Scarseth 1994). In Shamanism, the shaman plays a critical role. The basic ideals of the shaman are as follows: The shaman is thought to be capable of entering supernatural realms or dimensions in order to obtain answers to the problems of their community; the shaman is physically present in the natural world, but at the same time enters into another dimension, enabling travel of the soul; the shaman has many travels in this other dimension, and some travels are to bring guidance to misguided souls, to separate evil spirits from human souls, or to alleviate the soul of all elements acting upon it to cause illness; the shaman affects the spiritual world, which in turn affects the natural world; the shaman brings balance to a soul; and the creation of balance results in the elimination of the ailment, thus restoring health for the human body. In other words, shamans are thought to treat ailments and illnesses by mending the soul.

An individual does not decide to become a shaman. Hmong tradition maintains that shamans are chosen and given special gifts by spirits. When an individual is chosen, it is believed that they have no choice but to become a shaman. If one chooses to not become a shaman, sickness or misfortune will come to that individual or that individual's family, so chosen individuals usually follow through and become a shaman to avoid this. A shaman may be a male or female. Many traditional Hmong will seek the advice of shamans for treatment of illness or disability.

It is important that recreation therapists not assume that all shamans are alike. Most shamans are unique and are given special gifts and talents. For example, one shaman might be very talented in healing burns, while another shaman's gift may be in mending broken bones. Working with shamans will often be part of good medical practice to provide what is required to best meet the client's needs. In practice it might not be all that different from working with Christian ministers praying for the health of their congregations.

In many cases, only life-threatening situations will cause Hmong families to seek help from healthcare institutions like hospitals in the U.S. Instead, Hmong may seek the advice of a shaman. This is not due to a lack of trust in medical authorities. It is an issue of belief. Seeking help from a shaman is usually the first step, because as previously mentioned, the Hmong are very spiritual. When they get sick, it is believed that the cause of the sickness is a spirit or spirits. By performing a shamanic ritual, a shaman is believed to be able to identify the cause of a problem. Once the problem has been identified, the next step is to call the soul back to the original body. At this point, the shaman will bargain with spirits in the supernatural world to give back an individual's soul. If the individual becomes well after a few days or weeks, another ritual will be performed to thank the spirits, sometimes by sacrificing an animal. Shamans are also sought out before hospitals because many Hmong also believe that when sicknesses or misfortunes happen within a family, it is because spirits are trying to send the family a message. For example, the spirit message could mean that someone in the family has done wrong, and this must be addressed. Traditional Hmong also do not believe in donating organs, because they believe that this will prevent the spirit of the dead person from going free and reincarnating (Eliade 1964).

Therapeutic recreation specialists need to be aware of a number of traditional Hmong cultural beliefs that mat may impact professional practice.

Holidays, Celebrations, and Recreation

Hmong New Year

The Hmong New Year is the favorite celebration and the only holiday the Hmong have that is their own. Traditional custom indicates that the Hmong New Year is a time of rest from the harvest season, and psychologically a time for the Hmong people to start new lives, a new year, or a new beginning. It is also a time to bring friends and family together and catch up with life. In Laos, the Hmong New Year may last up to two weeks (Roop & Roop 1990). Often in U.S. cities, celebrations last two or three days, often over a weekend. The celebration takes place in areas where large Hmong communities exist, and activities happen in modified forms in smaller Hmong communities.

This celebration frequently occurs in November and December (traditionally at the end of harvest season when all the farming work is completed), serving as a kind of Thanksgiving holiday for the Hmong people. At the Hmong New Year Festival, many Hmong will dress in traditional Hmong clothes and enjoy traditional Hmong food, dance, music, recreation, and sports.

Traditionally, the Hmong New Year celebration is a time for young people to meet their potential future mates. A ball toss game called *pov pob* is traditionally played. In this game, young women and young men who may be considering marriage line up facing each other and begin by throwing a tennis-ball-sized ball back and forth. Girls can toss the ball with other girls or boys, but boys can't toss the ball with other boys. Participants are not allowed to toss the ball with members of their own clan who are the opposite sex. During the game, a player who misses or drops the ball must give up an item, such as accessories or part of their outfit, to the player who threw them the ball. Items are recovered by singing love songs to the person who possesses their item. More recently, participants have been allowed to use recorded music to play their favorite love songs for one another.

Next are a few other practices, games, or activities the Hmong might observe during their New Year celebration (or during other times), including:

- *Soul Calling* — Calling back every soul in the family to unite with the family by performing a ritual from a shaman.
- *Rubber band game* — This is a rubber band jump rope played by younger children in Thailand and Laos. In this game, rubber bands are looped together to create a long elastic cord (often up to ten feet long). To begin this game, there should be a minimum of three participants. The rubber band jump rope is stretched between two children. Each child holds one end while the third player jumps over it, using more difficult rule challenges for each level. For example, at one level, the player will have to jump over the rubber band on one foot without touching or getting their foot tangled in the rubber band.

This game is very close to the game Limbo. In Limbo, players must go under the bar without touching it or knocking it down, while in the rubber band game, players must jump over the rope as the height increases. After each successful leap, the jump rope is raised higher and higher until the player touches the cord, then another player takes a turn.

- *Spear, cloth, and rock* — This game is similar to the well-known rock, paper, and scissors. In this version, rock beats spear, spear beats cloth, and cloth beats rock.
- *Pebble Jacks* — Similar to the U.S. version of the game Jacks; however, the Hmong version does not involve a ball. The object is to toss a pebble into the air, and as the pebble is still up in the air, the player must grab the pebbles on the ground and also grab the thrown pebble before it hits the ground, all with the same hand. At level one, the player must toss one pebble in the air and grab one pebble on the ground. At the second level, the player must grab two pebbles on the ground and catch the tossed pebble. Level three increases with one more pebble on the ground, and this continues on through the different levels.
- *Spinning Tops* — Spinning tops is a game played by Hmong boys and men. Any number of people can play the game. For safety reasons, all players must stand behind a starting line. (Traditional spinning tops were carved from a very hard wood, and flying tops can be dangerous.) The first player or the first team will set their tops spinning about ten feet in front of the starting line. The second player or second team will throw their top to try and hit the first player or first team's already spinning tops. Once a top is hit, the player whose top spins the longest is the winner. If the second player or team does not hit the first player's or team's spinning top, that player is out. If the first player or first team's tops fall first, that player is out until the next round. Play continues until everyone on the first team is out, then the teams change positions.

- *Extreme Volleyball* — This is very much like traditional volleyball, but without using the hands. Players will use high kicks, flips, and different techniques to get the ball over to the other side.
- *Sewing* — Women and girls sew for leisure and sometimes for money to help the family.

Conclusion

This section has addressed demographic data, significant historical information, general cultural group information, basic treatment implications, and holidays and celebrations of Hmong Americans. Although all information provided will not provide complete insight to all Hmong Americans, it may be used as a basic tool for better understanding this cultural group as it relates to recreation therapy service delivery.

Portions of the previous information on Hmong culture and games were based on interviews conducted by a Hmong undergraduate student participating in the McNair Scholars Program at the University of Wisconsin-La Crosse. Interviews were conducted with Hmong college students, parents, and elders in La Crosse and Wisconsin Rapids, Wisconsin during spring and summer 2011.

References

Bertrais, Y. 1978. *The Traditional Marriage among White Hmong of Thailand and Laos*. Chiangmai, Thailand: Hmong Center.

Campbell, T. & Chang, B. C. 1981. Health Care of Chinese in America. In *Transcultural Health Care*, edited by G. Henderson & M. Primeaux, 162-171. Reading, MA: Addison-Wesley.

Culhane-Pera, K. A & Xiong, P. 2003. Hmong Culture: Tradition and Changes. In *Healing By Heart: Clinical and Ethical Case Studies of Hmong Families and Western Providers*, edited by K. Culhane-Pera, D. E. Vawter, P. Xiong, B. Babbitt, & M. M. Solberg, 11-68. Nashville, TN: Vanderbilt University Press.

Eliade, M. 1964. *Shamanism, Archaic Techniques of Ecstasy, Bollingen Series LXXVI*, 3-7. New York: Pantheon Books.

Hoeffel, E., Rastogl, S., Kim, M., & Shahid, H. 2012. The Asian Population: 2010. 2010 Census Briefs. Retrieved from www.census.gov/prod/cen2010/briefs/c2010-br-11.pfd. Assessed July 2, 2012.

Jungen, Anne. 2013. Man Charged with Threatening Woman Who Refused Abortion. *La Crosse Tribune*, March 5.

Lowenstien, A. & Glandville, C. L. 1995. Cultural Diversity and Conflict in the Health Care Workplace. *Nursing Economics 13*: 203-209.

Mattison, W., Lo, L., & Scarseth, T. 1994. *Hmong Lives from Laos to La Crosse: Stories of Eight Hmong Elders*. La Crosse, WI: The Pump House.

McInnis, K., Petracchi, H., & Morgenbesser, M. 1990. *The Hmong in America: Providing Ethnic-Sensitive Health, Education, and Human Services.* Dubuque, Iowa: Kendal/Hunt Publishing Co.

Roop, P. & Roop, C. 1990. *The Hmong in America.* Appleton, WI: Appleton Area School District.

Smolan, R. & Erwitt, J. 1994. *Passage to Vietnam: Through the Eyes of Seventy Photographers*. Hong Kong: Against All Odds Productions and Melcher Media.

Yang, K. 2012. Hmong Contemporary Issues. www.hmongcontemporaryissues.com. Accessed September, 2012.

10. Mexican Americans

Mexican Americans are U.S. citizens who trace their national origin to Mexico or who are native-born Americans with Mexican parents. The Census 2010 counted 31,798,258 Mexican Americans. Mexican Americans account for about 63% of the Hispanic or Latino population in America, up from 58% in 2000. The majority of Mexican Americans live in the West (51.8%), followed by the South (34.4%), then the Midwest (10.9%), and finally the Northeast (2.9%) (Ennis, Rios-Vargas, & Albert 2011). The top five states with the most Mexican Americans are California, Texas, Arizona, Illinois, and Colorado.

Mexican Americans are considered by many to be part of Latino culture. Latinos, who are also known as Hispanics, comprise the largest and fastest-growing ethnic minority group in the U.S., a distinction they have had for several decades. In 2006, the U.S. Census indicated the Hispanic population was 44.3 million (or 14.8 percent of the total U.S. population). Recently, Latinos have surpassed African Americans as the largest minority group in the U.S. In 2010, the U.S. Bureau of the Census counted 50,477,574 Hispanics, accounting for 16.3% of the total U.S. population (Ennis et al. 2011). The Census Bureau estimates by the year 2050, Hispanics will account for more than half of the U.S. population (Ennis et al. 2011).

Latinos have, as with other ethnic groups, made important achievements in every American arena including the arts, science and technology, politics, law, finance, sports, and journalism. Many well-known Latinos have had a significant impact in the U.S., including Supreme Court Judge Sonia Sotomayor; deceased actor/musician Desi Arnaz; singers Charo, Joan Baez, Linda Ronstadt, and Ricky Martin;

Antonia Novello (U.S. Surgeon General during the first Bush administration); Henry Cisneros (former mayor of San Antonio and HUD Secretary in President Bill Clinton's administration); Henry Gonzalez (former Texas representative for the House of Representatives); Mary Joe Fernandez (former tennis great); and actors Anthony Quinn, Rita Hayworth, Rita Moreno, and many others.

Regardless of their success in America, many of us know little about our Latino neighbors, their culture, their history, or their diversity. Latino history goes back further than American history. People of Spanish ancestry explored America centuries ago: Hernando de Soto discovered the Mississippi River in 1541, while Francisco Vasquez de Coronado explored the American West in 1540.

The term "Hispanic" is derived from *Espana* — Spain — the country that led the conquest of the New World. For the sake of clarity, Spanish Latin America is composed of Cuba, Puerto Rico (which is a U.S. Commonwealth, not a sovereign nation), the Dominican Republic, Panama, Venezuela, Colombia, Ecuador, Peru, Bolivia, Chile, Argentina, Uruguay, and Paraguay. All citizens and residents of the U.S. who originated from these nations or have ancestral roots from these countries are known as Hispanics. However, the term "Hispanic" is not accepted by all groups; "Latino," "Chicano," "Mexicano," "Mexican American," "Spanish-American," or "La Raza" (known to some as "The Race"), and others may be preferred by some people. The Census Bureau also includes Spanish Americans — individuals whose forebears came directly from Spain — among Hispanics, but many scholars limit the definition to those of Spanish Latin American origin.

Perhaps no other ethnic group in America is as diverse in its culture, physical appearance, and traditions as Hispanics. Having roots in so many different nations, each with its own distinct culture, history, indigenous language(s), religions, culinary traditions, and individual philosophies makes Hispanics a very diverse group. Although Hispanics may share some common characteristics, there are distinct differences between and within different groups.

In Spanish-speaking Latin America, people may not refer to themselves as Hispanic (many prefer the term "Latino"). Each country is a wonderful melting pot of diverse peoples. Nationality takes priority above other things. Thus, Mexicans call themselves *Mexicanos*, Puerto Ricans refer to themselves as *Puertorriqueños*, Cubans call themselves *Cubanos*, and so on. It is noteworthy that all these immigrants are grouped under the Hispanic collective because most identify more with the sub-group to which they belong. *Chicano* is an abbreviated form of *Mexicano*, the Spanish word for "Mexican," and was originally a pejorative term used by both whites and Mexican Americans to refer to Mexican-born unskilled workers in the U.S., particularly recent immigrants. However, since prejudice seldom makes fine distinctions among those of similar characteristics, Mexican Americans have often been labeled Chicano. Now, as with African Americans and the civil rights agenda, many Chicanos assert their ethnic pride in the word Chicano.

Some Important Historical Dates for Mexican Americans

The histories of Mexico and the U.S. are very closely intermingled. When we speak of Mexican Americans, we do not mean an ethnic minority who merely crossed our borders and then by slow assimilation became American. Mexico controlled most of the southwestern and western U.S. before it became part of the United States. Many Mexican Americans trace their roots to Mexican families that became Mexican American when the U.S. claimed the lands from Mexico. As a result, some Mexicans have a saying: "We never crossed the border — the border crossed us."

The original lands of Mexico were inhabited by many different ethnic Indian groups, including the Mayas and Aztecs. However, like much of South and Central America, the Indians were overthrown and colonized by Spain from 1521 to 1810. This colonization led to both the acquisition of Spanish culture and the loss of parts of the original cultures. In 1776, the U.S. colonies declared themselves independent of

Europe. By 1810, the Mexican *Criollos* — or Creoles, those born to Spanish parents in Mexico — were ready to follow suit. Led by Father Miguel Hidalgo y Costilla, in 1810 the native peoples and those of mixed native and Spanish heritage, who had suffered terrible discrimination, rebelled against the Spanish rule. Mexico acquired its independence from Spain in 1810.

The current United States-Mexican border extends from the mouth of the Rio Grande River in Texas to the Pacific Ocean — about 2,000 miles. The border was established as the result of the 1848 Treaty of Guadalupe Hidalgo, which ended the Mexican-American War (as it is referred to in the U.S.) or the American Intervention (as it is known in Mexico) (Ehrlich, Bilderback, & Ehrlich 1979). In ending the Mexican-American war, Mexico conceded the current lands of Texas, New Mexico, California, Arizona, Nevada, Utah, and half of Colorado to the United States.

Historical and continued friction between those of Mexican descent and Americans have characterized the Mexico-America border and Mexican-American and American relations due to many issues. The issues include Mexican opposition to slavery in Texas while Mexicans provided assistance to escaping slaves in the 1850s; the massacre of Americans at Santa Ysabel in 1916; the incursion of U.S. troops into Mexico during the 1870s; the influx of American investors into Mexico in the 1920s; the expropriation of American-owned oil companies in Mexico during the late 1930s; the introduction of U.S. agribusiness in Mexican farming in the 1940s, 1950s, and 1960s, with disastrous results; and U.S. immigration policy (Ehrlich et al. 1979; Samora 1971). In addition, Americans currently have issues with controlling illegal immigrants from Mexico.

When Santa Anna's forces stormed the Alamo and killed 182 Texans, Anglo and U.S. hatred against Mexico and anything Mexican exploded with a vengeance, and the seeds of ethnic prejudice and intolerance spread throughout the United States. The period between 1920 and 1950 was especially troublesome for Mexican Americans. In

1924 U.S. immigration laws were put into place. Northern Europeans were the favored immigrants, while Southern Europeans were allowed limited immigration. Almost all Asians were excluded as legal immigrants. However, no quotas were established for the Western Hemisphere, so Mexico became the largest supplier of inexpensive labor for U.S. companies. Many who fled Mexico for the U.S. after the Mexican Revolution were just happy to have a job, no matter how tough the job was. Yet in the U.S., many lived in *barrios/colonias*, Latino neighborhoods (immigrant ghettos) that provided some semblance of the old country. Essentially, a barrio was home away from home for those of Mexican descent.

In the 1920s, the Great Depression was looming and significant numbers of Americans became unemployed while wages dropped significantly for others. Many of the places Mexicans worked came to a halt. As a result, Mexican immigration to the United States declined. President Franklin Roosevelt, trying to help the situation, initiated efforts to put many Americans back to work, including the Works Project Administration of 1935. Subsequently, a repatriation movement deported as many as one-half million Mexicans in the 1930s.

However, during World War II, when the U.S. needed more workers, the repatriation efforts were reversed, bringing more Mexicans back to the U.S. This resulted in a bitter experience for Mexicans who had been sent home when not needed and then brought back when their services were required.

The Chicano movement emerged from the unrest fomented by the Vietnam War and the African American civil rights movement in the 1960s. Many prominent Mexican Americans were instrumental in advancing Mexican American rights, including Cesar Chavez, the famous Mexican American civil rights labor worker, who did much to propel the Chicano movement. The movement involved education about Mexican American rights and injustices, while urging Mexicans to fight for their rights as American citizens. Another legend of the movement, Reies López Tijerina, who was born in Texas, organized the Federal

Alliance of Land Grants in 1963. This movement demanded millions of acres of land be returned to the descendents of original Mexican owners. Still another legend of the movement was Rodolfo "Corky" Gonzalez, who founded the Crusade for Justice, which addressed social ills in Mexican American communities. Finally, Texan José Angel Gutiérrez established Mexican Americans United in 1970, which sought to end discrimination against Chicanos by helping them gain access to mainstream politics and financial institutions.

Mexican American Culture and Customs

For Mexican Americans, the family is at the heart of the social structure. Mexican American families have traditionally been somewhat large, especially those residing outside large metropolitan areas. However, the extended family is as important as the nuclear family, since the entire family provides a sense of stability. Mexican families maintain close communication and gather often to celebrate holidays and family events. *Familismo* is an essential concept in Mexican American culture and means that family is primary and more important than individuals (Juarez, Ferrell, & Borneman 1998; Liberman et al. 1997). Family members have a strong sense of responsibility to each other within the family unit and are closely tied by affection, respect, loyalty, and unity. All members are expected to abide by these principles.

Tradition indicates that the father is head of the family and the central decision-maker, while mothers are greatly respected and admired. Men are expected to provide for and be in charge of their families. Though increasing numbers of women work outside the home, homemaking is women's customary role. In public, women are expected to show respect and submission to their husbands.

Recreation therapists should be aware that other family members, particularly males, may be involved in patient care decision-making. The therapist should encourage this involvement and include the family as a resource in care planning. Such adherence complies with traditional family gender roles.

As previously mentioned, gender roles are well defined for those of Mexican ancestry. Mexican American men are traditionally characterized by *machismo*, which refers to being proud, having virility, sexual prowess, strength, independence, bravery, and decision-making power. Machismo literally means "masculinity." Men with machismo may not reveal what might be considered the soft emotions such as fear, disappointment, or sadness. It is important for Mexican American men to appear strong. Machismo also involves demonstrating love and affection for the family and protecting them from harm. Within this concept males are expected to protect the family's reputation (Ramirez 1993).

Marianismo, meanwhile, describes the female role. Marianismo encompasses chastity, virginity, and sacredness. Females are expected to be devoted to their homes and family while sacrificing other interests. Marianismo acknowledges that women accept their fate as mothers and wives and be willing to endure for the good of the family (Gil & Inoa-Vazquez 1996). Nevertheless, mothers within the Mexican American community tend to enjoy a high social status. More specifically, research has shown that Mexican American women consider motherhood a desirable and respectable role and are likely to leave jobs and careers to take care of themselves during pregnancy and their children as they grow up (Lagana 2003). However, as Hispanic families become more and more acculturated to the American value of individualism, it may create cultural struggles for Mexican American women.

Recreation therapists should remember that machismo and marianismo may have both positive and negative attributes and distinct connotations for different individuals. As such, it may be considered inappropriate to speak to the wife before the husband when both are present, or fail to ask if the father or oldest male agree with a recommendation or plan — even if the male is not at the session. These concepts may have little or no influence for some, while for others the concepts' impact can be significant in understanding the patient/client.

Respect, or *respeto*, is another important element in Mexican American culture. For Mexican Americans, respeto involves a sense of admiration granted because of an intrinsic quality of an individual regardless of social, political, or financial standing. Respeto may also be granted to a person because of hierarchical standing, similar to how subordinates respect a supervisor (Chong 2002). In short, Mexican Americans desire respect in their relationships. They show deferential behavior, or respeto, to those who are older, male, of higher socioeconomic status, and positions of authority.

As Mexican Americans value respeto regarding authority figures, the recreation therapist may find it uncommon for Mexican Americans to be aggressive or assertive in patient-therapist interactions. Direct disagreement with therapists can be rare. As such, a response to a decision that the person or family disagrees with might be silence or noncompliance. The therapist may also find that Mexican Americans, adhering to respeto, may use limited verbal expression to the therapist as an authority figure. The patient/client may nod their head when the therapist speaks, but this may not necessarily mean agreement, only that the message has been heard or understood (Thillet-Bice 2006).

Recreation therapists should recognize that machismo, marianismo, and respeto can be interrelated in a rehabilitation context. In order to be perceived with respeto, the recreation therapist should understand and comply with the family and gender roles of machismo and marianismo. For example, respeto is enhanced when a patient enters the recreation therapist's office and the therapist stands up, walks over, and greets the patient, gesturing for the patient to sit down (in order to make the patient feel more comfortable). Likewise, a handshake is also a good way to end patient interactions; this also helps to build respeto. When discussing treatment, the therapist should be sensitive to the possibility that there may be concerns that are not expressed out of respect. Careful probing and giving the family permission to speak may bring out these issues.

Another important Mexican cultural element is *personalismo*. Personalismo may influence a Mexican American individual to be more likely to trust and cooperate with a recreation therapist who they feel is personable. Personalismo refers to the importance of personal contact (Chong 2002) and relating on a personal level. Personalismo implies a certain degree of informality in social situations and indicates enjoying the company of others and engaging in pleasant conversation. It is based on the knowledge of an individual's qualities that have been learned and accepted by another person over time.

It is important for recreation therapists to establish a personable relationship with Mexican Americans. A Mexican American might not establish a relationship with an institution or organization; however, the individual might establish a relationship with an individual from that organization. Seeing a familiar recreation therapist for each visit/session is a way of establishing personalismo. Also, asking the right kinds of questions may assist in establishing personalismo. For example, asking a female about her life, her spouse, and her children can go a long way in establishing personalismo.

Close communication practices aid in establishing this important Mexican American value. Personalismo is the human quality of being able to relate on a personal level, regardless of social or financial standing (Chong 2002).

Religion is also a centerpiece of Mexican culture. In general, the majority of Hispanics self-identify as Catholic (Castex 1994), although a small percentage are Protestants and Jews. As Catholics, Mexicans show devotion to Our Lady of Guadalupe, or Mary the mother of Jesus, who they believe protects them and intervenes on their behalf. The Virgin Mary is considered their patron saint after she appeared to Juan Diego on December 12th more than four hundred years ago. This day continues to be celebrated annually. Mexican Americans may have a fatalistic view of life similar to the religious views of African Americans (Soriano 1994).

In other words, they believe that people must face and accept the inevitability of their fate because it is God's will.

This fatalistic view could pose challenges for the recreation therapist, because patients/clients may view disability — and possibly the after-effects of disability — as "meant to be," and therefore not seek ways to improve their quality of life. If this occurs, the recreation therapist could say, "You are in rehabilitation for a reason. You were meant to be helped."

In addition to understanding Mexican American family and religion traditions, recreation therapists should seek to better understand Mexican American interpersonal communication practices. Communication and the relationship between the patient/client and the recreation therapist are significant keys to providing quality care. Language barriers can pose serious communication problems; Spanish is the primary language spoken by most Hispanics (although there are a number of different dialects and variations). However, some will speak English as well. In some households, Spanish is spoken at home by the parents but not the children. Sometimes only the first generation read, write, and speak Spanish; the second generation may speak Spanish but not read or write it; and the third generation may understand Spanish but only speak, read, and write English (Thillet-Bice 2006). Obviously it is beneficial to have Spanish-speaking staff.

It is wise for recreation therapists to know everyday Spanish terms which may assist when communicating with Mexican Americans who speak Spanish. Here are some basic terms and their meaning:

English	Spanish
Good morning	Buenos días
Good afternoon	Buenas tardes
Good	Bueno
Bad	Malo

I am sorry	Lo siento
Yes	Sí
No	No
Excuse me	Perdóname
Thank you	Gracias
How are you?	Cómo está usted?
You're welcome	De nada
Good-bye	Adiós
Today	Hoy
Please	Por favor
I am sorry I do not speak Spanish	Perdóname, no hablo español

Understanding nonverbal communication is also very important for recreation therapists working with those of Mexican ancestry. Physical touch by strangers and casual use of first names is not appreciated early in relationships (De Paula, Lagana, & Gonzalez-Ramirez 1996). However, formality may decrease over time as warmth in communication increases.

It is desirable for recreation therapists during initial encounters to address Mexican Americans with formal titles such as Mr., Mrs., Miss., Ms., or Señor, Señora, or Señorita. The recreation therapist should understand that in Mexican culture, a title signifies respect.

Personal space and touch are also important. Mexican Americans communicate through physical contact and appreciate physical closeness, as they frequently kiss, shake hands, and embrace family members (Chong 2002). Most Mexican Americans maintain closer personal space than many other Americans during conversations or when interacting with family, friends, and healthcare professionals (Thillet-Bice 2006). If a recreation therapist maintains increased spatial distance, Mexican Americans may perceive this as indicating insensitivity or a lack of interest (Flores et al. 2000). In order to demonstrate interest during communication, Mexican Americans may stand in close proximity and touch the other person as they converse.

Direct eye contact is less common among those with Mexican ancestry than among others. Some Mexican Americans do not maintain eye contact when conversing, especially with someone considered an authority figure. This is considered disrespectful (Thillet-Bice 2006). However, recreation therapists recognize that establishing eye contact is important in patient-therapist interactions. Eye contact from the therapist can demonstrate *respeto* for the patient, concern for what the patient is saying, and sense of caring. It is possible to overdo eye contact, especially with patients/clients of the opposite gender. For example, too much direct eye contact can be considered aggressive between two men and flirtatious between men and women.

Recreation therapists must try to find the amount of eye contact that is considered appropriate.

Holidays, celebrations, and recreation

Mexico is a country with lots of celebrations. Although there are only seven national holidays in the country, many Mexican villages and parochial sections of the country have their own celebrations, and most are either religious, historical, food, or personally based. Consequently, Mexican Americans may observe a number of traditional celebrations because they have ties with villages in Mexico. Some cities and towns in the U.S. with a sizeable Mexican population have their own special holidays celebrating patron saints, which combine Spanish, Aztec, Maya, Pueblo, and other native cultural and religious elements. Below are six significant events that Mexican Americans may celebrate.

El Día de los Muertos (the Day of the Dead)

The Day of the Dead is a holiday celebrated primarily in Mexico and by people of Mexican heritage in the United States and other countries. The holiday, celebrated on November 1st and 2nd, gathers family and friends to pray for and remember friends and family members who have died. In conjunction with the Catholic holy days of All Saints' Day and All Souls' Day, the Day of the Dead includes building altars honoring the deceased, eating the favorite foods of the departed, and visiting or bringing gifts to grave sites (Moehn 2000).

This holiday has gained more prominence around the world in places such as Brazil, the Philippines, Spain, Africa, and the United States, as Mexican communities outside of Mexico have grown both numerically and economically. In Mexico, November 1st is used to honor deceased children, whereas November 2nd is the day for honoring adults. In some parts of Mexico, people may spend the entire night beside the graves of their relatives (Doldson-Wade 2002; Harris, Williams, & Woo 1998).

There is no strict, uniform way that this holiday is carried out. There many variations, including telling stories of the dead, poem reading, dancing, dressing up as the deceased, and so on.

Los Posadas

One of the most festive holiday periods for Mexicans is Christmas. Christmas in Mexico is first and foremost a religious holiday. Christmas festivities begin with Las Posadas, which is Spanish for "The Inn." Las Posadas consists of nine continuous days of processions and parties beginning on December 16th and ending on December 24th. Las Posadas typically involves processionals with both children and adults. The first procession generally depicts the journey of Joseph and Mary to find a place to stay for the night. Participants portraying Joseph or Mary carry a doll representing the Christ child. Processions usually lead to a designated private home or some central location. Typically, at the first and second locations (as prearranged), the holy family is turned away. At a predetermined site, the pilgrims are told that there is no room in the posada (inn), but they can stay the night in the stable. Then the doors are opened and all are invited to enter. Scriptures are read and Christmas carols are sung. The event is an active way of teaching children the story of the nativity. However, the major attraction is the merrymaking that follows: the celebration ends with the breaking of a piñata. Children break the piñata with a stick and eagerly gather up its contents. The doll is left at the chosen site and picked up the next night when the processional begins again. The holiday festivities culminate on *Noche Buena* (Christmas Eve) with the celebration of a late night Mass. After this, the families head home for a traditional Christmas supper. The evening concludes with opening Christmas gifts. Because these celebrations may last into the wee hours of the evening, December 25th is set aside as a day to rest and enjoy the leftovers from Noche Buena (Silverthorne & Ellis 1992; Williams 2003; Winchester 1996).

Cinco de Mayo

One of the most popular Mexican holidays in the United States is Cinco de Mayo (Spanish for "May 5"). In Mexico, Cinco de Mayo is primarily a regional holiday celebrated in the Mexican state of Puebla. There may be only limited recognition of the holiday in other parts of Mexico. In fact, Cinco de Mayo is not even a federal holiday in Mexico. Public and government offices and banks remain open. Cinco de Mayo marks the victory of the Mexican Army over the French at the Battle of Pueblo. The battle actually occurred on May 5, 1862. Although the Mexican army was eventually defeated, the Battle of Pueblo came to represent an important symbol of Mexican unity and patriotism; Mexico had demonstrated to the rest of the world that it was willing to defend itself against foreign takeovers (Mattern 2006; Otto & Alamillo 2008; Silverthorne & Ellis 1992).

In the United States, the Battle of Pueblo came to be known as simply "5 de Mayo," and many people equate it wrongly with Mexican Independence Day, which actually occurred on September 16, 1810. Incrementally, Cinco de Mayo has become very commercialized, and many people view it as a time for celebration. However, Cinco de Mayo tends to be more of a Chicano holiday than a Mexican one, and it's celebrated on a much grander scale in the U.S. than in Mexico. Many people of Mexican descent in the U.S. celebrate Cinco de Mayo by having parades, music, dancing, and other types of festive events. Cinco de Mayo is probably best recognized as a date to celebrate the culture and experiences of Americans with Mexican ancestry, much like St. Patrick's Day is for the Irish, Chinese New Year is for the Chinese, and Oktoberfest is for the Germans. Other people, regardless of their ethnic origins, observe and participate in these kinds of celebrations.

Diez y Seis de Septiembre (Mexican Independence Day from Spain — Sept 16th)

Diez y Seis de Septiembre is an important national patriotic holiday in Mexico. On this day, people of Mexican heritage all over the world celebrate Mexico's independence from Spain. On September 16th, 1810, Father Miguel Hidalgo y Castilla launched the Mexican War of Independence against Spain (Silverthorne & Ellis 1992). The struggle with Spain centered on the rights of *Criollos* (Creoles) with Spanish ancestry who were born in the New World, but who were not given the same privileges as those born in Europe.

Semana Santa (Holy Week)

In Mexico, Easter is a combination of *Semana Santa* (Holy Week — Palm Sunday to Easter) and *Pascua* (Resurrection Sunday until the following Saturday). Semana Santa is Mexico's second most important holiday season of the year, behind Christmas. For many Mexicans, this two-week period is the time for vacation — not necessarily for traveling, but rather for staying close to home and enjoying the company of the immediate community (Silverthorne & Ellis 1992; Williams 2003).

Semana Santa celebrates the last days of Christ's life, while Pascua celebrates Christ's Resurrection. In many communities, the full passion play is superbly costumed and enacted from the Last Supper, the Betrayal, the Judgment, the Procession of the Twelve Stations of the Cross, the Crucifixion, to finally the Resurrection.

Feast of Our Lady Guadalupe

The patron saint of Mexican Americans is Our Lady of Guadalupe. On December 12th, the day of Our Lady of Guadalupe is celebrated in Mexico and the United States. In Mexico City at the beautiful basilica of Our Lady of Guadalupe, large processions enter with flowers, banners, and singing (Harris, Williams, & Woo 1998; Winchester 1996). This is a festive day for families as they gather for parties where food and piñatas are focal points. Traditional piñata shapes for this occasion include donkeys, for the donkey that carried the Virgin Mary; fish, symbolizing Christ; and birds, representing those that sang when Mary appeared to Juan Diego.

Mexican Cultural Symbols

In addition to the previously described celebrations, Mexican Americans have symbols which are important in Mexican culture. The following three items are representative of Mexican American heritage.

El Charro and Charreada

El Charro, a man on horseback, has been a relatively long-standing visual representation of independent Mexico since the 1831 revolution. El Charro is the Mexican version of the American cowboy, arising from the ranch culture first brought to Mexico by the Spanish.

The *charreada* is a rodeo. In the rodeo, El Charro shows off individual skills with a rope while displaying his decorative and elegant costume. The charreada is a festive event that incorporates equestrian competitions and demonstrations, costumes and horse tricks, music, and food. Currently, the charreada includes men who compete in roping and riding events, and women who execute feats and precision maneuvers while riding horses (Reilly & Jermyn 2002).

In the United States, the charreada is a way for Mexican Americans to express pride in their Mexican heritage. The atmosphere created by the events, costumes, music, and food provides Mexican Americans an opportunity to celebrate their identity while culturally connecting them to Mexico. Perhaps more important, it is a time when family members and communities can be together, celebrating their heritage and identity.

Mariachi

Mexico has a rich musical tradition with many popular musical genres. One of the most popular Mexican musical genres is *ranchera*, which is interpreted by a band of mariachis. Mariachi is a type of musical group, usually consisting of violins, trumpets, and Mexican guitars. The musicians dress in elaborate traditional Mexican outfits with wide-brimmed hats (Gonzalez 2005; Collins 2007).

Mariachi goes beyond music. It is the sum of a cultural revolution expressed through musicians dressed in popular traditional clothing — *charro* suits — which encompass the essence of Mexico and its people. This is something cultural, spiritual, and traditional that is unique to Mexico.

Mariachis play at a number of events, including weddings and other formal occasions such as a *quinceañera* (a girl's fifteenth birthday celebration), and mariachis are often used to serenade women because many of the songs played touch the heart of the opposite sex. Other songs may be sad or indicate someone appreciates another's company.

The Pinata

Although having traditions in many regions of the world, the piñata has become a noted part of Mexican tradition and is used mainly in Mexican celebrations. The history of the piñata is filled with legend and folklore. Legends of the piñatas are many and include being used as offerings to Aztec gods, as a lure for conversion by Spanish missionaries, and as a symbol of hope hung above the head of the participants, symbolizing looking to the heavens, expecting a prize (Devlin 2012).

In Mexico, the piñata is used for both religious and fun festivities. Participants engage in the activity just for the fun of it and to bring an element of surprise and wonderment to parties when children are successful in liberating the goodies contained in the piñata. Piñatas are especially popular in Mexico during *Las Posadas* and at birthday parties. Singing is traditionally part of these celebrations. Children will sing, dance, and hop while attempting to break the piñata.

Today, piñatas can be found in all shapes and sizes. Modern ones often represent cartoon characters or other characters known to children. Others are shaped like fruits, rockets, baskets, and so on. Sometimes political figures are satirized, while at Christmas star-shaped piñatas suggestive of the Star of Bethlehem are very popular. Traditionally, piñatas are filled with candy and fruits.

Conclusion

This section has addressed selected demographic data, selected significant historical information, general cultural group information, basic treatment implications, and selected holidays and celebrations of Mexican Americans. Although the information provided will not provide complete insight to all Mexican Americans, it may be used as a tool for better understanding this cultural group as it relates to recreation therapy.

References

Castex, G. M. 1994. Providing Services to Hispanic/Latino Populations: Profiles in Diversity. *Social Work 39*: 288-296.

Census Briefs. Retrieved September 14, 2011, from http://www.census.gov/prod/cen2010/briefs/c2010br-04.pdf.

Chong, N. 2002. *The Latino Patient: A Cultural Guide for Health Care Providers*. Yarmouth, ME: Intercultural Press.

Collins, C. 2007. *What is the Mariachi?* Retrieved July 16, 2012, from www.mexconnect.com/articles/1875-what-is-the-mariachi.

Delvin, W. 2012. *History of the Pinata*. Retrieved April 15, 2012, from www.mexconnect.com/articles/459-history-of-the-pinata%c3%B1ata.

De Paula, T., Lagana, K., & Gonzalez-Ramirez, L. 1996. Mexican Americans. In *Culture and Nursing Care*, edited by J. G. Lipson, S. L. Dibble, & P. A. Minarik, 203-221. San Francisco, CA: UCSF Nursing Press.

Doldson-Wade, M. 2002. *El Dia De Los Muertos*. Georgetown, TX: Children's Publishing. USA.

Ehrlich, P. R., Bilderback, L., & Ehrlich, A. H. 1979. *The Golden Door: International Migration, Mexico, and the United States*. New York: Ballantine Books.

Ennis, S. R., Rios-Vargas, M., & Albert, N. G. 2011. *The Hispanic Population: 2011*.

Flores, G., Abreu, M., Schwartz, I., & Hill, M. 2000. The Importance of Language in Pediatric Care: Case Studies from the Latino Community. *Journal of Pediatrics 137*: 842-848.

Gil, R. M. & Inoa-Vazquez, C. 1996. *The Maria Paradox: How Latinas Can Merge Old World Traditions with New World Self-esteem*. New York: G. P. Putnam.

Gonzalez, S. 2005. *History of the Mariachi*. Retrieved July 16, 2012, from www.mariachi.org/history.html.

Harris, Z., Williams, S., & Woo, Y. 1998. *Piñatas and Smiling Skeletons: Celebrating Mexican Festivals*. Berkley, CA: Pacific View.

Juarez, G., Ferrell, B., & Borneman, T. 1998. Perceptions of Quality of Life in Hispanic Patients with Cancer. *Cancer Practice 6*(6): 318-324.

Lagana, K. 2003. Come Bien, Camina y No Se Preocupe — Eat Right, Walk, and Do Not Worry: Selective Biculturalism During Pregnancy in a Mexican American Community. *Journal of Transcultural Nursing 14*: 117-124.

Liberman, L. S., Stoller, E. P., & Burg, M. A. 1997. Women's Health Care: Cross-cultural Encounters Within the Medical System. *Journal of the Florida Medical Association 84*(6), 364-373.

Mattern, J. 2006. *Celebrate Cinco De Mayo*. Berkley Heights, NJ: Enslow Publishing.

Moehn, H. 2000. *World Holidays: A Watts Guide for Children*. New York: The Rosen Publishing Group, Inc.

Otto, C. & Alamillo, J. 2008. *Celebrate Cinco De Mayo*. Washington, DC: National Geographic.

Thillet-Bice, F. 2006. Cultural Consideration for the Latino/Hispanic Client. In *Developing Cultural Competence in Physical Therapy Practice,* edited by J. B. Lattanzi & L. D. Purnell, 209- 237. Philadelphia, PA: F. A. Davis Company.

Ramirez, R. L. 1993. *Dime Capitan: Reflexiones Sobre la Masculinidad*. Rio Piedras, Puerto Rico: Ediciones Huracan.

Reilly, M. & Jermynm L. 2002. *Cultures of the World: Mexico.* New York: Benchmark Publishers.

Samora, J. 1971. *Los Mojados: The Wetback Story.* Notre Dame, IN: University of Notre Dame Press.

Silverthorne, E., & Ellis, J. 1992. *Festival: Mexico's Greatest Celebrations.* Brookfield, CT: Millbrook.

Soriano, F. I. 1994. Latino Perspective: A Sociocultural Portrait. In *Managing Multiculturalism in Substance Abuse Services*, edited by J. U. Gordon, 117-144. Thousand Oaks, CA: Sage.

U.S. Bureau of the Census. (1990). *Current population reports* (Series p-20, No. 499 (3).

U.S. Bureau of the Census Race and Ethnicity Classification. Available at: http://census.gov/population. Accessed July 4, 2010.

Williams, C. 2003. *The Festivals of Mexico.* Philadelphia, PA: Mason Crest.

Winchester, F. 1996. *Hispanic Holidays.* Mankato, MN: Bridgestone.

11. Puerto Rican Americans

Puerto Rican Americans are U.S. citizens who trace their ancestry to the island of Puerto Rico. Because of Puerto Rico's commonwealth status, Puerto Ricans are unique; they are born as naturalized American citizens. Therefore all Puerto Ricans, whether born on the islands of Puerto Rico or in the mainland U.S., are Americans. Puerto Rican Americans are the second largest Latino group in America, far behind Mexican Americans. The Census 2010 counted 4,623,716 Puerto Ricans in the U.S. mainland (Ennis, Rios-Vargas, & Albert 2011). The majority reside in New York (about 900,000). Many Puerto Ricans migrated to the mainland between 1947 and 1957 and settled in East Harlem and Upper Manhattan, which became known as Spanish Harlem. Most Puerto Ricans live in New York, California, and Texas (Klor de Alva 1998). However, increasing numbers reside in all U.S. states, with many living in Florida, New Jersey, Massachusetts, and Connecticut.

Puerto Rico is often improperly called a country. It is actually a commonwealth and is under U.S. laws. Its residents are American citizens but are barred from voting in U.S. presidential elections. Puerto Ricans do not pay federal income tax. Puerto Rican people are very proud of their land, heritage, and their Afro-Spanish traditions.

Despite the presumed advantages of American citizenship, Puerto Ricans are overall one of the most economically disadvantaged Latino groups in America. Many Puerto Rican communities are plagued by the same problems as most minority-group communities: poverty, poor education, and high crime rates. Also, since most Puerto Ricans are of mixed Spanish and African descent, they tend to deal with discrimination similar to that experienced by African Americans. Such bias can be

187

compounded by a lack of English-speaking proficiency. Finally, because of a long history of intermarriage among Spanish, Indian, and African ancestry groups, Puerto Ricans are probably among the most ethnically and racially diverse groups in the world. With such diversity, there is significant variance in skin color, economic sufficiency, political thought, and so on.

Some Important Historical Dates for Puerto Rican Americans

The Commonwealth of Puerto Rico (the official name) is about a thousand miles southeast of Miami and is an island (although the commonwealth also includes several other smaller islands), measuring about a hundred miles long and thirty-five miles wide. Puerto Ricans call their island *Borinquen,* meaning the land of the brave lord (Klor de Alva 1998). The Taíno, the indigenous inhabitants of the island, named it. Christopher Columbus, on his second voyage in 1493, discovered and took control of the island in the name of Spain. The Taíno welcomed the Spanish conquistadors with open arms, believing them to be gods. However, soon they regretted it. They were enslaved as the Spanish looked for gold. Mistreated and even murdered, those that survived rebelled, and subsequently many were killed or ran to the hills for safety. In 1508, the Spanish granted settlement rights to Juan Ponce de León, who became the first governor. Workers were needed, so Ponce de León brought in African slaves to work the land. African slavery persisted in Puerto Rico until 1873. By then, Africans had grown deep roots and Puerto Rico was their home.

The United States occupied Puerto Rico in 1898 after the Spanish-American War, and changed the name of island to Porto Rico. The spelling was discontinued in 1932 and changed to Puerto Rico. Puerto Ricans consider themselves a distinct Caribbean people, regardless of their official U.S. citizenship. At times, there is no strong opposition to U.S. citizenship; rather, there continues to be a desire for association with the United States due to some of the benefits of being U.S. citizens.

Puerto Rican American Culture and Customs

Puerto Rican customs, traditions and beliefs — especially for the least acculturated — are influenced by Puerto Rico's Afro-Spanish history. Many of the treatment implications identified with Mexican Americans may also be applied to Puerto Rican Americans. Although most Puerto Ricans can be rather strict Catholics, local island customs often add a Caribbean flavor to some Catholic ceremonies. Like many other Caribbean islanders, Puerto Ricans believe in *espiritismo*, the notion that the world is populated by spirits who can communicate with the living through dreams.

> *Recreation therapists should be aware that some Puerto Rican clients may believe in spirits. Therapists might consider adjusting their treatment and rehabilitation to accommodate such beliefs.*

Puerto Ricans can be described as a festive people, and many customs involve socializing, food, and drink. Puerto Rican people are famous for throwing large, elaborate parties with music, dancing, food, and drinking to celebrate cultural events.

Puerto Ricans may also be described as a passionate ethnic group. Much of this passion can be seen in traditions that dictates how people should interact with one another. Friendliness is a part of Puerto Rican culture. For example, like in many other Latino cultures, it is considered an insult to turn down a beverage offered by a friend or stranger. It is also customary for Puerto Ricans to offer food to guests in their homes.

> *Recreation therapists should carefully consider their informal interactions with Puerto Rican clients; polite refusals and acceptances of invitations and offers can help establish effective client-patient relationships.*

Puerto Ricans may also adhere to other traditional beliefs and superstitions, such as not eating in front of pregnant women without offering them food for fear that they might miscarry, that marrying or starting a journey on a Tuesday is bad luck, and that dreaming of water or tears is a sign of impending heartache or tragedy.

Recreation therapists should take into consideration that Puerto Ricans may have traditional beliefs and superstitions that may have an impact on their treatment and rehabilitation.

Most Puerto Ricans are of Spanish ancestry. Although the U.S. controls Puerto Rico, Spanish is the main language on the island of Puerto Rico, though many Puerto Ricans do speak English. During the 1950s, there was a significant increase in Puerto Rican immigration to the U.S. mainland. Thousands of islanders moved to New York City and other large cities in search of jobs and a better life. Consequently, many Puerto Ricans living in the U.S. may speak both languages, while others may speak Spanish only.

Recreation therapists should be aware that an interpreter might be needed for effective communications with Puerto Ricans.

Puerto Ricans consider family life a fundamental core cultural value. The family remains an important, lasting, dependable support network. Although the divorce rate is high among Puerto Ricans, most prefer married life. Remaining single has become increasingly acceptable, but marriage is still considered an important indicator of successful adulthood. The nuclear family is most important for Puerto Ricans; however, other relatives often actively participate in child rearing and family decisions. Sharing household chores between working spouses is becoming more common, but raising children is still predominantly a female role, even among the more family-oriented men. Male authority is respected and expected.

Child rearing and family are important in Puerto Rican culture. Traditionally, husbands and fathers are heads of households, and older male children are expected to be responsible for younger siblings, especially females (Green 2102). The concept of *machismo*, as described with Mexican Americans, is a highly regarded value for Puerto Rican men.

Puerto Rican mothers are the central figures in child rearing. When the mother is not available, relatives (including aunts, uncles, cousins, grandparents, and godparents) may be considered part of the immediate family and are preferred to people outside the family sphere. Consequently, professional care providers are looked on with ambivalence. From infancy, children are socialized towards family and community participation. Traditionally, children are expected to learn through observation rather than instruction. While boys are raised to be more aggressive, girls are raised to be more quiet, and all children are expected to learn *respeto*, one of the most valued traits in Puerto Rican culture. As described with Mexican American children, respeto refers to a belief that everyone has intrinsic dignity that should never be transgressed. Within this belief is the idea that people must respect others by learning to respect themselves. Other highly valued qualities such as obedience, industriousness, and self-assurance will follow when a child gains respeto.

Just like with respeto, the concept of education is equally important to Puerto Rican culture. A traditional understanding of education is that it refers to formal schooling. However, in Puerto Rican culture, an educated person is one who is respectful, cordial, courteous, and polite — not necessarily one who has received formalized book learning. This not to say that formal education is not important. More recently, having credentials has become more important, and as a result more Puerto Ricans are earning high school and more advanced degrees.

Also important to Puerto Rican culture is the concept of directness. Puerto Ricans tend to believe directness is rude; they often prefer people who are publicly expressive but not excessively so.

Recreation therapists should be aware that too much assertiveness on the part of the therapist may negatively impact effective patient-therapist relationships.

Holidays, Celebrations, and Recreation

Puerto Ricans celebrate many traditional U.S. Christian holidays like Christmas, Easter, and New Year's Day in addition to other traditional Puerto Rican holidays and celebrations. The majority of Puerto Ricans are Catholic, so they celebrate many religious observances of the Roman Catholic Church.

Día de los Tres Reyes Magos (Three Kings Day)

Día de los Tres Reyes Magos is celebrated on January 6th. Tradition has it that on the feast of the Epiphany, the three kings, bearing gifts, visited the newly born Christ child in Bethlehem. This tradition is repeated and reflected today with the belief that on this day the three kings will visit every good child to deliver gifts. Custom has it that on the eve of the Epiphany, children collect hay, straw, or grass and place it in boxes, containers, or on their shoes placed under their beds. This gesture is a gift of food for the kings' horses while they rest between deliveries. If a child has been good for the past year, he or she will receive candies, sweets, or toys. If the child has misbehaved or has been naughty, he or she would instead find a lump of dirt or charcoal in their box.

Día de los Muertos (Day of the Dead)

Día de los Muertos (Day of the Dead) is celebrated November 1st and 2nd. On these days, Puerto Ricans celebrate and honor their deceased ancestors. The celebration is based on the belief that there is interaction between the living world and the world of spirits. The spirits of the dead are said to come back for family reunions. Many celebrate the Day of the Dead by setting up shrines in their homes to honor the memory of deceased loved ones and to welcome their visiting souls. Others visit their loved one's cemetery plot and decorate it with flowers, candles, and food. The holiday is celebrated with family and community gatherings, music, and feasting, and the festivity of its observance acknowledges death as an integral part or life.

Día de los Innocentes (Day of the Innocents)

Día de los Innocentes is celebrated after Christmas on December 28th. It has been celebrated for more than 150 years. The Day of Innocents, similar to April Fool's Day, is a day for practical jokes and fooling others. During the day, groups of friends might totally cover their cars and trucks with elaborate frilly decorations and wear head-to-toe costumes. It is customary to play practical jokes on others. In Puerto Rico, the day typically ends with a parade with decorated floats full of loud noise and brilliant colors.

El Día de la Candelaria (Candlemas Day)

Candlemas is celebrated on February 2nd. This ancient festival marks the midpoint of winter, halfway between the shortest day and the spring equinox. Candlemas also is an old Christian festival that celebrates the birth of Jesus. On this day, all the candles that will be used in the church during the coming year are brought into church and a blessing is said over them. On this day there are colorful parades, dances, and festivities. There is a candlelit procession to the local churches, and large parties and bonfires with food and drinks with family, friends, and loved ones.

Quinceañera (Coming out party - 15th birthday)

Quinceañera is celebrated on a young girl's fifteenth birthday. The celebration embraces religious customs and the virtues of family and social responsibility. The Quinceañera tradition celebrates the young girl (la Quinceañera) and recognizes her journey from childhood to maturity. The customs highlight many aspects of the young woman's life, including God, family, friends, music, food, and dance. The Quinceañera celebration traditionally begins with a religious ceremony. A reception is held in the home or a banquet hall. The festivities include food and music, and in most gatherings, a choreographed waltz or dance performed by the Quinceañera and her court. It is traditional for the Quinceañera to choose special friends to participate in what is called the Court of Honor. Usually, these young people are her closest friends, her brothers, sisters, cousins — the special people in her life with whom she wants to share the spotlight. The Quinceañera's Court of Honor can be comprised of all young girls (called Dama), all young men (called Chambelán or Escorte or Galán), or a combination of both. The Quinceañera traditionally wears a ball gown, with her court dressed in gowns and tuxedos. Guests usually receive small tokens to commemorate the celebration.

There are many traditions throughout the Quinceañera celebration. One of the most popular is the Changing of the Shoes. The father or favored male relative ceremoniously changes the young girl's flat shoes to high heels. This is a beautiful symbol of the Quinceañera's transformation from a little girl to a young lady.

The Quinceañera may also involve a church ceremony in which a special "kneeling pillow," sometimes personalized with the Quinceañera's name, is placed in position for the young girl to kneel on during the ceremony. A touch of elegance is added with smaller decorated ceremony pillows for the presentation of the Quinceañera's ceremonial gifts. At the reception, there is usually a toast to the Quinceañera, known as the *brindis*. With decorated champagne glasses, the guests are invited to offer their congratulations and best wishes.

Sometimes a "last doll" is used as part of the ceremony or as a decoration and keepsake. In some customs, the Quinceañera doll represents the last of her childhood, now that the Quinceañera will focus on the things of a young lady.

Santería (Religion)

Santería is a prominent religion practiced by many Puerto Ricans. Santería is a combination of religious traditions or beliefs of older African and Catholic traditional religions. However, Santería is not a religion of a book, like Judaism, Christianity, or Islam. Like many aboriginal religions, it is preserved by an oral tradition. It is thought to have originated in Cuba and Brazil. Very little official information about beliefs, rituals, symbolism, and practice is known or released to the general public. One has to be initiated into the faith before information is freely released to a participant-believer. The religion is thought to be a combination of the traditional African Yoruba Faith and the worship of Catholic saints. Yorubans are members of a West African community based in the region of southwest Nigeria.

Santería is thought to be a vibrant nature religion based on reading stones, seashells, water, and herbs, as well as other natural objects. The African Yoruba slaves, who brought the religion from Africa, identified the Orishas (spiritual beings or presences that are interpreted as one of the manifestations of God) with the Catholic saints in order to preserve their African religions. Those who practice Santeria recognize the saints as having the same natural powers as the Orishas for healing and spell-casting.

Practitioners of Santería believe in one creative force called Olodumare. The Orishas are worshipped not as gods but as spirit guardians who offer divine guidance and protection to reverent followers. It is believed that every individual in the Santería religion has a personal Orisha to help them along the path of life.

Conclusion

This section has addressed demographic data, significant historical information, general cultural group information, basic treatment implications, and selected holidays and celebrations of Puerto Rican Americans. Although the information will not provide complete insight to all Puerto Rican Americans, it may be used as a tool for better understanding this cultural group as it relates to recreation therapy.

References

Aponte-Pares, Luis. 1998. What's Yellow and White and Has Land All Around It? Appropriating Place in Puerto Rican Barrios. In *The Latino Studies Reader: Culture, Economy, and Society,* edited by Antonia Darder & Rodolfo Torres, 271-280. Malden, MA: Blackwell Publishers, Ltd.

Castex, G. M. 1994. Providing Services to Hispanic/Latino Populations: Profiles in Diversity. *Social Work 39*: 288-296.

Chong, N. 2002. *The Latino Patient: A Cultural Guide for Health Care Providers*. Yarmouth, ME: Intercultural Press.

Ehrlich, P. R., Bilderbackm L., & Ehrlich, A. H. 1979. *The Golden Door: International Migration, Mexico, and the United States*. New York: Ballantine Books.

Ennis, S. R., Rios-Vargas, M., & Albert, N. G. 2011. *The Hispanic Population: 2011*. 2010 Census Briefs. Retrieved September 14, 2011, from http://www.census.gov/prod/cen2010/briefs/c2010br-04.pdf.

Darder, A. & Torres, R. 1998. Latinos and Society: Culture, Politics, and Class. In *The Latino Studies Reader: Culture, Economy, and Society,* edited by Antonia Darder & Rodolfo Torres, 3-26. Malden, MA: Blackwell Publishers, Ltd.

De Paula, T., Lagana, K., & Gonzalez-Ramirez, L. 1996. Mexican Americans. *Culture and Nursing Care,* edited by J. G. Lipson, S. L. Dibble, & P. A. Minarik, 203-221. San Francisco, CA: UCSF Nursing Press.

Flores, G., Abreu, M., Schwartz, I., & Hill, M. 2000. The Importance of Language in Pediatric care: Case Studies from the Latino Community. *Journal of Pediatrics 137*: 842-848.

Flores, J. 2000. *From Bomba to Hip-Hop: Puerto Rican Culture and Latino Identity*. New York: Columbia University Press.

Gil, R. M. & Inoa-Vazquez, C. 1996. *The Maria Paradox: How Latinas Can Merge Old World Traditions with New World Self-esteem*. New York: G. P. Putnam.

Green, D. (2013). Puerto Rican Americans. Retrieved from http:www.everyculture.com/multi/Pa-Sp/Puerto-Rican-Americans,html. on December 8, 2012.

Juarez, G., Ferrell, B., & Borneman, T. 1998. Perceptions of Quality of Life in Hispanic Patients with Cancer. *Cancer Practice 6*(6), 318-324.

Klor de Alva, J. 1998. Aztlan, Borinquen, and Hispanic Nationalism in the United States. In *The Latino Studies Reader: Culture, Economy, and Society,* edited by Antonia Darder & Rodolfo Torres, 68-83. Malden, MA: Blackwell Publishers Ltd. Malden, MA.

Liberman, L. S., Stoller, E. P., & Burg, M. A. 1997. Women's Health Care: Cross-Cultural Encounters within the Medical System. *Journal of the Florida Medical Association 84*(6): 364-373.

Moehn, H. 2000. *World Holidays: A Watts Guide for Children.* New York: The Rosen Publishing Group, Inc.

Quinceanera Traditions, Sweet Sixteen Traditions. 2010. *Quinceanera Dresses, Sweet 16 Invitations, Quinceanera Ideas, Quinceanera Traditions.* Accessed March 2. http://www.quinceanera boutique.com/quinceaneratradition.htm.

Thillet-Bice, F. 2006. Cultural Consideration for the Latino/Hispanic Client. *Developing Cultural Competence in Physical Therapy Practice,* edited by J. B. Lattanzi & L. D. Purnell 209-237. Philadelphia, PA: F. A. Davis Company.

Reilly, M. & Jermyn, L. 2002. *Cultures of the World: Mexico.* New York: Benchmark Publishers.

Soriano, F. I. 1994. The Latino Perspective: A Sociocultural Portrait. In *Managing Multiculturalism in Substance Abuse Services,* edited by J. U. Gordon, 117-144. Thousand Oaks, CA: Sage.

U.S. Bureau of the Census. (1990). Current population reports (Series p-20, No. 499 (3).

U.S. Bureau of the Census Race and Ethnicity Classification. Available at: http://census.gov/population. Accessed July 4, 2010.

Winchester, F. 1996. *Hispanic Holidays.* Mankato, MN: Bridgestone.

About the Author

Jearold Holland is an Associate Professor in Therapeutic Recreation at the University of Wisconsin — La Crosse (UW-L). Dr. Holland has more than 30 years teaching experience in higher education and teaches courses in Therapeutic Recreation and Recreation Management at UW-L. While at UW-L, Holland has served the institution in many capacities including Chair of the Department of Recreation Management and Therapeutic Recreation, Graduate Program Director, President of the Multicultural Faculty and Staff Organization, Assistant Football coach, and has served on numerous university committees and assignments.

Before UW-L, Dr Holland was Director of Therapeutic Recreation at Wyalusing Academy where he developed and implemented a comprehensive therapeutic recreation program to meet the needs of emotionally disturbed and physical disabled adolescents. He was also Child Care Unit Coordinator at St. Michael's Home for Children.

Dr. Holland's research interests include therapeutic recreation, recreation for underrepresented groups, community recreation, and higher education. Dr. Holland has made numerous presentations on underrepresented groups in therapeutic recreation, recreation, and higher education at the local, state, and national level. He is also the author of *Black Recreation: A Historical Perspective* and co-author of two urban novels *Twisted* and *Nadine's Revenge*.

Jearold and his wife Theresa live in La Crosse, Wisconsin. They have three children, Bradley, Mackenzie, and Lukas.